Berthold Lubetkin's Highpoint II and the Jewish Contribution to Modern English Architecture

In 1935, the Russian-born Jewish architect Berthold Lubetkin and his firm Tecton designed Highpoint, a block of flats in London, which Le Corbusier called 'revolutionary'. Three years later, Lubetkin completed a companion design. Yet Highpoint II felt very different, and the sense that the ideals of modernism had been abandoned seemed hard to dispute. Had modern architecture failed to take root in England?

This book challenges the belief that English architecture was on hiatus during the 1930s. Using Highpoint II as a springboard, Deborah Lewittes takes us on a journey through the defining moments of modern English architecture – the 'high points' of the period surrounding Highpoint II. Drawing on Lubetkin's work and his writings, the book argues that he advanced influential, lasting theories which were rooted in his design for Highpoint II.

Lubetkin's work is explored within the context of wider Jewish emigration to London during the interwar years as well as the anti-Semitism that pervaded Britain during the 1930s. As Lewittes demonstrates, this decade was anything but quiet. Providing a new perspective on twentieth-century English architecture, this book is of interest to students and scholars in architectural history, urban studies, Jewish studies, and related fields.

Deborah Lewittes is an Assistant Professor of Art History at the City University of New York, USA. She has been a research fellow at the Courtauld Institute, London, UK, and Tufts University, Massachusetts, USA, and was a Lecturer at the Parsons School of Design at The New School, New York, USA.

This incisive study greatly adds to our understanding of early key monuments of Modernist architecture. But its principal value lies with the way it deals with the intersection of architectural debates with some of the wider cultural-political trends of the 1930s and 1940s, namely with the notion of the 'diaspora of Modern architects' as being largely identical with a 'diaspora' of Continental Jewish architects. Finally, the context can also be expanded to the new 1950s theories of 'English' architecture. A most necessary and timely book.

Stefan Muthesius, Honorary Professor, School of Art, Media and American Studies, University of East Anglia, UK

Deborah Lewittes deftly interweaves three narratives neglected by previous architectural scholars: the design of a controversial London housing project by the radical and troubled Russian émigré architect Berthold Lubetkin; the history of modernist architectural culture in England in the 1930s; and a reflection on diasporic Jewish identity in an endemically xenophobic and anti-Semitic context. An original, provocative, and revisionist study.

Joan Ockman, Distinguished Senior Lecturer, School of Architecture, University of Pennsylvania, USA

Berthold Lubetkin's Highpoint II and the Jewish Contribution to Modern English Architecture

Deborah Lewittes

LONDON AND NEW YORK

First edition published 2018
by Routledge
2 Park Square, Milton Park, Abingdon, Oxon, OX14 4RN

and by Routledge
711 Third Avenue, New York, NY 10017

Routledge is an imprint of the Taylor & Francis Group, an informa business

British Library Cataloguing-in-Publication Data
A catalogue record for this book is available from the British Library

Library of Congress Cataloging-in-Publication Data
Names: Lewittes, Deborah, author.
Title: Berthold Lubetkin's Highpoint II and the Jewish contribution to
    modern English architecture / Deborah Lewittes.
Description: First edition. | New York : Routledge, 2018.
Identifiers: LCCN 2018009195 (print) | LCCN 2018019366 (ebook) |
    ISBN 9781351124386 (eBook) | ISBN 9780815357452 (hardback)
Subjects: LCSH: Highpoint II (London, England) | Lubetkin, Berthold,
    1901-1990—Criticism and interpretation. | Tecton (Firm) | Highgate
    (London, England)—Buildings, structures, etc. | London
    (England)—Buildings, structures, etc. | Jewish architects—England. |
    Architecture and society—England—History—20th century.
Classification: LCC NA7863.G72 (ebook) | LCC NA7863.G72 L645 2018
    (print) | DDC 720.942/09043—dc23
LC record available at https://lccn.loc.gov/2018009195

ISBN: 978-0-8153-5745-2 (hbk)
ISBN: 978-1-351-12438-6 (ebk)

Typeset in Times New Roman
by Swales & Willis Ltd, Exeter, Devon, UK

To Leo

Contents

Figures

Acknowledgments

With (alphabetical) thanks to my wonderful teachers and mentors: Danny M. Abramson, Carol Armstrong, Rosemarie Haag Bletter, Michael Cadden, Romy Golan, Christopher Green, Rose-Carol Washton Long, and Kevin D. Murphy. I also thank Ruth Bass and Joanna Merwood-Salisbury for their support.

With grateful appreciation to the organizations that funded this research over the years: the Kress Foundation, the Andrew W. Mellon Foundation, the Paul Mellon Centre for British Studies, and the PSC-CUNY Research Foundation.

I also thank the Society of Architectural Historians of Great Britain for a generous publication grant and the Department of Art and Music at the City University of New York, Bronx Community College, for travel funds. The publication of this work has been supported in part by Historians of British Art, an affiliated society of the College Art Association.

With additional thanks to my dear friends Ayako, Sukey, Paul, Jin, and Kumi.

And finally, indescribable gratitude to my parents, the kindest and most encouraging people I know, and to Edward Eigen, merci pour tout.

Figure 0.1 Highpoint II, façade, canopy, and caryatids. Photo: Leo Eigen.

Introduction

Just the Highpoints: London in the thirties

"England," Eric Mendelsohn wrote in 1934, "is an interregnum."[1] 1934 – the year after he was excluded, for being Jewish, from the Reichsbank competition in Berlin, was forced to flee Germany, and then moved to London. 1934 – the year of his father's eightieth birthday. His father, still in Germany as European Jewry collapsed around him in the country whose name Mendelsohn never again uttered after leaving. Sheltered in London, what must Mendelsohn have been thinking, knowing what was happening in his home country?

An interregnum. Was he referring to England in a general sense, as it existed alongside a continent growing increasingly unstable and hostile, unsure of the route his new homeland would take, but, at the moment, seemingly calm and separate from the growing horror and desperation? Or, as an architect, did he mean the state of English architecture, not quite embracing the experimental style of its continental European counterparts and instead operating on the margins of avant-garde activity? The same architecture scene had inspired Bruno Taut, Mendelsohn's colleague at the Arbeitsrat für Kunst and also Jewish, to observe several years earlier that England "seems to be pausing for breath, so far as creative architecture is concerned."[2] Taut fled Germany in the same year as Mendelsohn, first to Switzerland and eventually to Japan, putting into practice his European modernist ideals by teaching and designing industrial objects.

An interregnum and a pause – suspended moments. The two architects' words relay a similar feeling and are hardly fraught enough in light of the events in Europe framing their lives, though of course they could not have known the magnitude of what was to come. Perhaps Mendelsohn, a self-proclaimed Zionist, sensed England was, for him, a waystation before he could return to practicing on his own, which he did in the British Mandate of Palestine, a place he first visited and immediately loved, also in 1934. But before working in the Middle East and then making his way to the

United States, his gap years in England were spent in partnership with Serge Chermayeff, also a Jewish architect, born in Russia but raised in England from an early age. The collaboration was the result of a required government policy; émigré architects who wished to practice in England had to be taken under the wing of an already-established architect.

I begin with these architects because of their obvious and inarguable importance to the history of modern architecture; nobody can doubt Mendelsohn's or Taut's abilities to evaluate the architecture of their day. These two architects' biographies are also crucial, their migrations far from unique. Even though Taut did not land in London, the forced journeys the two took were typical of that extended moment's historical tragedy. Both help paint a complete picture of London in the thirties, when the undeniable backdrop is the decimation of Europe's Jewish communities and the resettlement of thousands of refugees. Mendelsohn, Taut, and thousands of others escaped and put down roots elsewhere, while millions of course did not.

What was this 1930s English world that Mendelsohn and Taut saw in suspension? In 1935, Le Corbusier saw things quite differently. Discussing London, he wrote of "the total transformation of architecture and town planning" in *The Architectural Review*.[3] The occasion for such spectacular language was Highpoint, a tower block of flats in the affluent Highgate section of north

Figure I.1 Highpoint I. Used with permission from RIBApix.

Figure I.2 Highpoint II. Used with permission from RIBApix.

London, designed by the Russian Jewish émigré architect Berthold Lubetkin (b. 1901, Tbilisi, Georgia; d. 1990, Bristol, UK) and his firm Tecton (Figure I.1).

For Le Corbusier, Highpoint, its international style sleekness rising from the winding lanes of the neighborhood that bordered Hampstead Heath, was a prototype, the "seed," he wrote, of an entirely new architectural example, full of promise and about to alter all of London. A mere three years later, in 1938, Lubetkin completed a companion Highpoint, a block of equally upmarket housing, on the adjacent site, yet it seemed to indicate that the architect had undergone a dramatic change of heart. Highpoint II cut a considerably different figure from Highpoint I, the first building's relative starkness now an ornamented assemblage of glass block and tile combined with earthy brick and classical caryatids, cast from the British Museum's collection of molds from the Erechtheum (Figure I.2).

J.M. Richards, the critic and editor of *The Architectural Review*, embraced Highpoint II's difference from the earlier work as "an important move forward from functionalism," prefiguring his own later renunciation of international style architecture. Few other modernists welcomed Lubetkin's changed course, and the fact that the course had indeed changed was hard to dispute.[4] Most saw Lubetkin retreating from his earlier architectural theories.

* * *

There are several intertwined threads that connect this study. First, I aim to counter Mendelsohn and Taut and their shared notion that modern British architecture in the thirties was on some sort of hiatus, "pausing for breath." Using Lubetkin's Highpoint II as a springboard, I will show that, in fact, there was much important activity during that time and that Lubetkin advanced influential, lasting ideals. Caryatids and all, Highpoint II will be placed within the so-called "interregnum" of the thirties to consider what it looks toward, as opposed to what it apparently retreats from. An understanding of Highpoint II will require us to take a synoptic journey through the defining narratives and important moments of modern English architecture – the high points, if you will, of the period surrounding Highpoint II, always linked back to Lubetkin, his work, and his writings. Second, and more largely, the overarching framework for this study is the significant (both in numbers and in impact) presence of European Jewish exiles and émigrés who settled in London in the late 1920s through World War II. We have already established that for some, such as Mendelsohn and Taut, emigration was a life-and-death necessity, while others, such as Chermayeff's family, were émigrés by choice, having left their homelands before the rise of Hitler. Lubetkin was less than forthcoming about certain aspects of his past, but he came to London in 1931, also by choice, via Paris, where he had worked in Auguste Perret's atelier. In all the émigrés' cases, foreignness marked these figures as outsiders in Britain, an identifying feature that prevented them from being fully absorbed in their new society. More specifically, being Jewish as well as foreign forced many to be doubly separate from British culture. Lubetkin went to great lengths to hide his Jewishness, and much bubbled beneath his ostensibly sleek surface; his daughter's 1995 autobiographical memoir *In this Dark House* recounts her discovery after his death that she was of Jewish heritage and that her grandparents, the architect's parents, had been killed in Auschwitz in 1940.

These sorts of realities define much of the cultural climate of 1930s England, which was anything but the quiet pause described by Mendelsohn and Taut. Even while Lubetkin thought he was successfully obscuring his Jewishness, fellow émigré architect Ernö Goldfinger, a Hungarian Jew, was hardly fooled, and thought of Lubetkin as a "scoundrel" for his attempted charade.[5] A lurking anti-Semitism pervaded the world of thirties Britain, and Lubetkin worked within that world. My intention, then, is to link these various strands of exploration. Highpoint II was deeply political, and

Lubetkin's architectural practice mattered long past the thirties. That decade itself was a time of activity and urgency, during which the landscape of modern London took shape, propelled by a strong Jewish impact.

Notes

1 Bruno Zevi, *Eric Mendelsohn* (New York: Rizzoli, 1985), 141.
2 Bruno Taut, *Modern Architecture* (London: The Studio, 1929), 203. This study will use England and Britain interchangeably. For an explanation of the convention, see the introduction to Michael Saler, *The Avant-Garde in Interwar England: Medieval Modernism and the London Underground* (New York and Oxford: Oxford University Press, 1999) or the first chapter of David Masters, "Constructions of National Identity: British Art 1930–1990" (Ph.D. diss., Open University, 1996).
3 Le Corbusier, "The Vertical Garden City," *The Architectural Review* 79 (January 1936): 9–10.
4 J.M. Richards, "Highpoint Number Two: Tecton, Architects," *The Architectural Review* 84 (1938): 166. Also see "Modern Flats in Highgate," in the same issue (161–4).
5 Nigel Warburton, *Ernö Goldfinger: The Life of an Architect* (London: Routledge, 2003), 73.

1 Building Highgate

High rises and uprisings

> . . . suppose [an architect] to set up the marble statues of women in long
> robes, called Caryatides, to take the place of columns . . .
>
> (Vitruvius, Book One, *The Ten Books on Architecture*)

We return, now, to the Highpoints. A mere three years before receiving the
commission for the first Highpoint, Lubetkin and six recent graduates of the
Architectural Association (AA) formed the collaborative firm Tecton. Lubetkin
had met the architect Godfrey Samuel, one of the six, through his roommate
in Paris, and Samuel in turn introduced Lubetkin to a group of students who
had gravitated toward each other at the AA, mainly in joint opposition to the
still-prevalent Beaux-Arts leanings of the AA's educational program, in spite
of the growing presence of vanguard voices. The name of the group derives
from the Latin (by way of Greek) word "architecton," meaning carpenter or
builder,[1] though certainly for Lubetkin, the name held additional significance;
"*Tektonika*" was used by Russian Constructivists to refer to a merging of the
ideological tenets of communism with the proper and functional use of industrial materials, and Lubetkin, we will discuss later, grew up amidst the heated
years and street protests of his Constructivist countrymen.[2] But there is still
another reference, to architectural tectonics; as discussed by Stanford Anderson:

> "*Tektonik*" referred not just to the activity of making the materially
> requisite construction . . . but rather to the activity that raises this con-
> struction to an art form . . . The functionally adequate form must be
> adapted so as to give expression to its function. The sense of bearing
> provided by the entasis of Greek columns became the touchstone of
> this concept of *Tektonik*.[3]

The tectonic, then, is the poetic expression of structural function, a concept
that will have resonance throughout our discussion of both Highpoints as

well as Lubetkin's later work. The most significant cultural implication of the firm, though, was not the etymology of its name, but rather the fact that Tecton was a collaborative architecture firm with shared, collective credit for its work, an unusual model for an English architectural practice during this time period. In England in the thirties, there was still a bourgeois air that surrounded the profession of architect; the organization of one's firm was not typically a site for experimentation. An architect trained and apprenticed according to set rules, so Tecton's approach was a strong rejection of the prevailing system.[4] Much later, in 1946, Walter Gropius founded TAC (The Architects' Collaborative), a move that inspired the title of Sigfried Giedion's 1954 book *Walter Gropius: Work and Teamwork*, but the convergence of the London-based Tecton architects in 1932 into a non-hierarchical cooperative was a new and different standard for the architecture world, typical of Lubetkin's desire to challenge the establishment.[5]

Highpoint – at the time of the initiation of the project, there were no plans for a second structure – originated when a wealthy Jewish industrialist, Sigmund Gestetner, commissioned Lubetkin to design communal worker housing for his employees in Camden Town, a crowded, fairly run-down neighborhood north of Regent's Park.[6] When the only appropriate site Gestetner could find was located in quiet, affluent, leafy Highgate, he altered the original program and asked Lubetkin to design flats to rent to middle- and upper-class tenants on the open housing market. The site chosen was accompanied by a set of zoning regulations, including a height limit on the street façade, which faces North Hill Road northeast of Hampstead Heath, and a restriction on developing the land to the building's rear. The resulting residential block, engineered by Ove Arup, is a symmetrical double-cruciform plan that rises seven stories on the street front and eight stories on the rear, garden-view side. A columned, curved *porte-cochère* faces the street, and the entire central bulk of the structure is raised on reinforced concrete *pilotis*; the upper residential floors each contain four two-bedroom flats and four three-bedroom flats. Ribbon windows in each flat are designed so that they can completely fold to the side, accordion-style, much to the chagrin of Lubetkin's engineer, allowing for a clear opening in the façade and melding indoor and outdoor spaces, thus "re-establishing contact with the garden in an off-the-ground flat."[7] A rooftop garden with its screen walls frames views and at the time, because of the building's hilltop location, was the tallest point in London. A radio aerial was placed on the roof, and although it is now altered, the original was modeled after the Vesnin brothers' 1923 design for the Palace of Labor, a deliberate Constructivist reference. Lubetkin, in fact, had studied with the Vesnins.

A series of communal spaces lead from the front entrance out to the rear garden. Most of the exterior of the structure is the neutral, seamless, near-unbroken white we have come to associate with the international style, what Le Corbusier called *le couleur-type*,[8] though there are elements that offer expressive relief. Curvilinear balcony walls, for instance, echo a curving wall of a ground-floor winter garden, and a curved ramp slopes down to the garden; Lubetkin inserted many sculptural elements such as these into his design, reminiscent of Le Corbusier's interpenetration of curves and diagonals into the modernist cube of Villa Savoye in Poissy (1929–30). The curves also call to mind Constructivist sculpture, as well as Lubetkin's own Penguin Pool, completed the previous year, which will be discussed later (Figure 1.1).

The exterior of the winter garden as well as the wall surrounding the front entrance are both faced in brown brick, a material that will be echoed in Highpoint II's cladding, and certainly refers to the curved stone wall of Le Corbusier's Pavillon Suisse in Paris (1930–2); Lubetkin, it must be said, was a master at absorbing and recontextualizing the design idioms of his day.

In what would become typical of Lubetkin's manner of presenting his work, every aspect of the design was explained in an extended series of drawings; the ones for Highpoint I were exhibited in 1934 at the Contemporary Industrial Design Exhibition. A group of architecture students had planned to come to the construction site, and Tecton wanted the rationale behind the design choices to seem clear, non-arbitrary, and scientific. Although much of

Figure 1.1 Highpoint I exterior: arabesque balcony parapets and curved exterior wall. Used with permission from RIBApix.

Highpoint's design truly did make use of rational, detailed analyses to maximize sunlight, views, and cross-ventilation within each flat, this was also largely a polemical exercise, in that the flats featured custom-designed fittings, far from *Existenzminimum*-influenced accommodations around which much modern architecture discussion of the day, at least on the continent, revolved. Furthermore, Highpoint included ground-floor flats for maids and porters, and a contemporary discourse on flats suggested that a lack of exterior access balconies marked it as more upscale than a block of workers' flats, the original undertaking, would have been.[9] Those who ended up living in Highpoint were "intellectual pace-setters," described by Howard Robertson of the AA as

> [t]hose who, for want of a better term, are anti-bourgeois, not politically but socially . . . artists, professional men, and generally those who through taste and education . . . enjoy the sensitive severity and restraint of a building such as 'Highpoint' . . . [and its] definite aesthetic intent.[10]

A year after Highpoint was finished, Gestetner hired Tecton to design a companion residential block on the adjacent site. The final structure, separated from Highpoint I by only six feet, is rectangular in plan and contains twelve two-story, four-bedroom residences. Despite the overall rectangularity of the footprint and the building, it is clearly delineated into three sections: a central block flanked by two symmetrical wings. As opposed to the generally unified, seamless surface of Highpoint I and the early machine aesthetic, the elevations of Highpoint II are more varied and expressive, reflect structural and functional differences, and emphasize the overall horizontality of the rectangular block, in spite of vertical accents. Tecton again collaborated with Arup, who devised the structural system. The central block uses a reinforced concrete frame with load-bearing walls,[11] which allowed the double-height living room walls in the central section on the rear of the building to be almost all glass – the windows are sixteen feet by ten feet – providing uninterrupted views out toward Hampstead Heath; the wings are built in the manner of a load-bearing wall system also used in Highpoint I. The cladding on the garden façade reflects this structural difference – the wings are solidly covered in cream tiles, appearing at first glance as unified as Highpoint I's seamlessness, while the central section appears lighter, almost as a glass and brick box projecting from the mass of the rest of the structure (Figure 1.2).

The cladding and structural differences also reflect different floorplans in the central section from those in the wings. Nonetheless, the windows and balconies in all three sections are aligned, giving a sense of unity to

Figure 1.2 Highpoint II rear elevation: central block and wing. Photo: Leo Eigen.

the elevation; they are also aligned with those on the rear elevations of Highpoint I, visually linking the two structures in spite of the very different footprints and details.

The street elevation is visually more complex. The front façade is aligned with that of Highpoint I, and as in the rear, the windows and balconies read continuously across the structures as well, in spite of the six-foot space between them (Figure 1.3).

The façade to an extent echoes the garden elevation, the wings in cream tile and the center block mainly in glass and brick, appearing to project outwards. The differentiation among the three sections is further emphasized by the vertical stair towers, expressed on the exterior by the use of glass-bricks, which had been used in abundance on the ground floor of Highpoint I and which are reminiscent of Pierre Chareau's 1932 Maison de Verre in Paris. In fact, all the materials used on the exterior of the second Highpoint had appeared on the façade of Highpoint I as well, but not in a way that indicated the underlying structure or function of the spaces, nor in a way that interfered with the overall effect of the elevation's seeming *couleur-type*. A ramp leading to the entranceway continues, unbroken, into the foyer, as if the glass wall and doorway separating the lobby from the driveway and front garden does not exist. Service lifts connected the kitchens with the

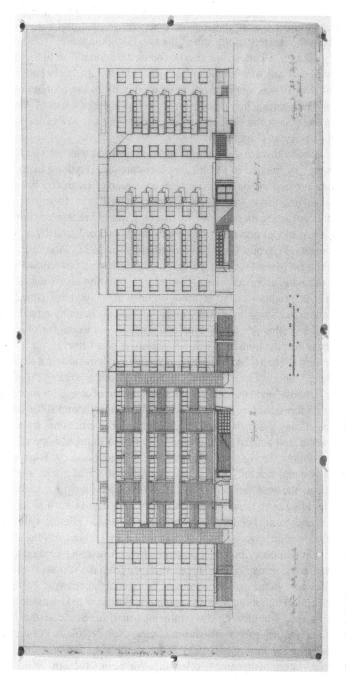

Figure 1.3 Design for Highpoint I and II, North Hill, Highgate, London: street elevations. Used with permission from RIBApix.

servants' quarters, suggesting accommodations even more upscale than the first apartment block, and lush gardens with a pool and tennis courts rounded out the entirety of the site of the two Highpoints.

Surely, though, all attention must be focused on and return to the curved *porte-cochère*. The loss of the seamless white exterior aside, the move from Highpoint I to II was summarized most succinctly in the aforementioned particular (and particularly) glaring element: Lubetkin's use of classical caryatids to suggest the support of the cantilevered canopy of the second building's entryway (Figure 1.4).

It was hard to discern a modernist message in what was seen as formalist game-playing, treated in the ensuing literature as everything from kitsch to irony to proto-postmodern historicism to a Marcel Duchamp-like found object to an impulsive *"jeu d'esprit,"*[12] and even harder to reconcile the apparently conflicting messages of the two buildings. One, a groundbreaking modern urban model according to Le Corbusier, seemed to deliver serious social content. Highpoint I had been inspired by the 1931 Narkomfin apartment building in Moscow, designed by Lubetkin's teacher and fellow Russian Jewish colleague, architect Mosei Ginzburg, a building also celebrated by Le Corbusier. Highpoint II was more whimsical, or perhaps conciliatory to reactionary leanings, or possibly audacious. Nobody quite agreed on an interpretation. Richards's aforementioned contentment aside, for other contemporary critics the transition was nothing short of a betrayal; far from the move forward Richards had described, orthodox modernists saw a step back. AA student Anthony Cox described a change in ethics, writing, "it is more than a deviation of appearance; it implies a deviation of aim . . . it is prepared to set certain formal values above use-values,"[13] and Highpoint II has come to be seen as closing a decade that brought a series of international style architectural works and activist architectural activities to London, none of which seemed to follow through on their initial radical implications. Highpoint II appeared emptied not only of the purist forms but of the social spirit that characterized the international style in Europe, clouding the intentions of the first building even though it too had decorative details, such as its aforementioned undulating balcony parapets, brightly painted interior walls in the ground-floor public spaces, rough brick detailing, and other curvilinear flourishes. The revolutionary potential discerned by Le Corbusier seemed to have evaporated, confirming England's great distance from the vanguards that had rallied elsewhere in the earlier decades of the twentieth century.

By the time Highpoint II was completed, World War II was imminent and the political situation on the continent was dire. Some of the Jewish émigrés were comfortably settled, but others, even Nikolaus Pevsner who had renounced his Judaism in 1921 and become a Lutheran, were forced into British internment camps, often just for being foreign. With many

Figure 1.4 Highpoint II detail of *porte-cochère* and caryatids. Used with permission from RIBApix.

of their members now in exile, the international artistic and intellectual communities had concerns more immediate and grave than the specifics of Lubetkin's *porte-cochère*, and the fading away of a minor moment of revolutionary fervor in England hardly mattered. Yet, the sort of about-face exemplified by Lubetkin's Highpoint II is largely responsible for the subsequent literature and narrative of modern British architecture, the consensus view holding that it was not much more than a compromised version of continental experiments, a movement that seemed to have produced disconnected instants of remarkable work rather than emerging from a larger cultural phenomenon. Highpoint I is seen as isolated and self-contained; William Curtis called it the swansong of the English movement in modern architecture, and others, such as John Summerson, openly doubted the lasting importance of Lubetkin.[14] A brief moment of architectural experimentation was gone in a flash, the thirties petering out into a new decade that also tends to be forgotten architecturally. The forties are first swallowed up by the war years, and then written off as populist styles converted even some prewar modernists. Much was published in *The Architectural Review* during this decade, documenting and discussing the move away from hard-edged modernism exactly as it was occurring.[15] We have already seen that Richards, for instance, who had written the important 1940 book *An Introduction to Modern Architecture* and had been an early supporter of the international style, began to argue against its abstract forms. Alison and Peter Smithson's design for Hunstanton Secondary Modern School (1954) in Norfolk, with its New Brutalist "warehouse aesthetic," apparently revived the radical energy of what had died out with the thirties generation and jumpstarted the postwar scene.[16]

While the egregiousness, or at the very least the incongruity, of Highpoint II's caryatids seem to suggest modernism in London was regressing by 1938, or perhaps never quite took root, considering Curtis saw it as already dying by 1935, the building's significance has nothing to do with finalizing or signaling an era in decline. As we will see, what Le Corbusier perceived in Highpoint I was far from abandoned in Highpoint II, and in fact, was a link to the postwar world that has become unyieldingly linked to the work of the Smithsons. With Highpoint II, Lubetkin, in fact, unwittingly calls into question the "fiercely uncompromising attitude" of the Team Ten generation.[17]

In his bitter response to Highpoint II, Cox remarked that the building "sits back on its haunches."[18] While Highpoint I, raised on modernist *pilotis*, had suggested physical lightness as well as social and architectural progress, Highpoint II seemed heavily weighted to the ground. One soared while the other watched sedentarily, Cox deciding the second tower block had given up on any sort of radical surge forward into the future. Even Richards had seen Highpoint I in terms similar to Cox's, writing dramatically in 1935:

"The revolution has arrived."[19] His analysis remained undeveloped – loose references to a machine-based "exactness" – but Le Corbusier's, that same year, was detailed. He explained what seemed significant about Highpoint, even though it was hardly the first international style work to be built in London, a city that he saw as having grown outward not upward, the terrible mess strangling the "modern spirit of the citizen." In Highpoint, Le Corbusier detected the implications of an entire urban theory that could fix London, Lubetkin's tower block clearly representing "the new tradition of vertical garden-cities."[20]

To invoke town planning took Highpoint out of the hermetic realm of luxury, where, with its servants' flats and generous spaces, it comfortably fit, and turned the focus towards its potential civic and wide-reaching significance, as well as a reality of thirties London: that the city desperately needed the sort of planning prototype to which Le Corbusier referred. Suburban sprawl in the London region is generally derided as a post-war catastrophe that degraded the English countryside and compromised the integrity of the metropolis – in the 1950s, *The Architectural Review* coined the derogatory term "subtopia" to criticize suburban sprawl – yet new waves of building had begun in the teens. Even in the twenties and long before the New Towns Act of 1946 became a scapegoat, architects and urbanists had recognized sprawl as a problem and condemned "ribbon development."[21] Linking Highpoint to overarching theories of urbanism reconceived it as more than an isolated building emerging from the leafy hills of north London, in spite of the literal fact that it was exactly that. In Le Corbusier's vision, additional tower blocks set within the open space surrounding Highpoint could redirect the course of urbanism in London and beyond. Standardization, communal services, the separation of automobile and pedestrian traffic, rooftop terraces; of course, Le Corbusier was propagating his own interests and seeing within Highpoint the ingredients his *Ville Radieuse* (Radiant City) comprised.

Le Corbusier had been exploring various forms of tower-in-a-park urbanism for more than a decade by the time Highpoint was unveiled, and for him, Highpoint suggested its future involvement in his iteration of a skyscraper city. Lubetkin had studied Le Corbusier, and Le Corbusier noticed; the latter's description of the effect of the *pilotis* and the flat roof on the functioning of Highpoint is especially elegant:

> the ground floor is no longer that part of the building usually sacrificed, where strangled rooms crowd around access corridors to the staircase . . . [It] extends like the superb surface of a lake, absorbing easily the lines of traffic of different speed and direction; the cars into their own door, pedestrians elsewhere, services elsewhere again.

Perambulators and bicycles have easy access, the cars are garaged in the right place. But more than circulation, this surface contains real parking spaces: a huge hall, full of light and air . . . leading with enormous virtuosity towards the two vertical services of stairs and lifts . . .

The top is no longer composed of an academic pitched roof folklore: it is a product of reinforced concrete. A great area of repose, broken only by wind-screens and shelters from the sun and rain which stand out against the sky. From the roof the view on all sides is incomparable: framed in concrete bays the whole sky appears, and the forests, and the garden suburbs, and the church spires, and the distant roads. A spectacle.[22]

For Le Corbusier, Highpoint contained the fundamental building blocks for his conception of the city. "By virtue of elevating everything on *pilotis* the ground surface would have become a continuous park in which the pedestrian would have been free to wander at will,"[23] with the rooftop, too, helping to provide the crucial modernist amenities of *espace, soleil, verdure*. Lubetkin's terms were different, but his allegiances seemed clear.

Highpoint attracted Le Corbusier, but it was not even Lubetkin's first triumphant work in London. It followed soon after Tecton's Penguin Pool (1934) in the London Zoo in Regent's Park, its curving ramps also having elicited enthusiastic responses from the progressive architectural community as well as the popular press (Figure 1.5).[24]

The clowning penguins were amusing, and critics embraced the pool as theater and playground, but its seriousness as architecture was not lost amidst the diversion. Later historians linked the spirals of the pool to Russian Constructivism, invoking El Lissitzky and Naum Gabo.[25] These associations are apt, and Lubetkin's connections to revolutionary Russia went beyond artistic forms and were deeper than his having merely been a witness to political turmoil. He was an art student in Moscow during the Russian Revolution, and grew up in a culture steeped in Russian Constructivism. He frequently asserted that the heroism of modern art was inseparable from Constructivism's social protests.[26] He tied the energy and activity of post-revolutionary Russia to the "dynamism of spiral architectural forms,"[27] inflecting the pool and its curves with the political content he was confident they contained anyway. Lubetkin studied with Konstantin Melnikov and considered Alexander Rodchenko to be "his mentor,"[28] and while Lubetkin was certainly not a major figure in the art movement, he is in fact a presence in Christina Lodder's canonical *Russian Constructivism*. Lubetkin's participation in agitprop street theater, most notoriously the 1918 re-enactment of the storming of the Winter Palace, is also documented, and such agit-impulses made their way with him to London. Lubetkin had also

Figure 1.5 Penguin Pool, London Zoo, Regent's Park, London: the elliptical pool and ramp. Used with permission from RIBApix.

enrolled in the free art workshops (SVOMAS) in Petrograd, formed after the Revolution, and studied in the VKHuTEMAS (Higher State Artistic and Technical Workshops) and INKhUK (Institute of Artistic Culture). If there is a running theme in his notebooks and private papers, it is that the heroism of modern art and architecture is rooted in the social protest art of Russian Constructivism, and that is the spirit with which he aimed to imbue his work. In 1932, Lubetkin wrote a two-part article for *The Architectural Review* on Soviet modern architecture and town planning, describing the energy and activity of post-revolutionary Russia.[29] The article talked about the "dynamism of spiral architectural forms," and in addition to the Penguin Pool and some elements in the Highpoints, the curve as a motif appeared often in his work for the remainder of his career.[30]

In 1936, the Museum of Modern Art (MoMA) in New York commissioned László Moholy-Nagy and Gyorgy Kepes to make a film, called *The New Architecture at the London Zoo*, about the Penguin Pool and other zoo buildings Lubetkin had designed. By then, both Moholy-Nagy and Kepes were living in London. Only Moholy-Nagy was Jewish, but both had fled their native Hungary. Lubetkin, ever argumentative, was apprehensive about the project, concerned that Moholy-Nagy's overriding interest in "the standpoint of pure visual perception" would misguide the film.[31] He instructed Moholy-Nagy that he wanted the film to be "a systematic account of the underlying reality. I doubted the value of a merely descriptive account of what happened, rather than why it happened, or what had to happen."[32] Neither Lubetkin nor MoMA was pleased with the film in the end. By this time Lubetkin had already established himself as a maverick and often sulphurous presence on the London architectural scene, freely criticizing the architectural establishment and his avant-garde colleagues alike, and he responded brusquely: "[a]s I had been afraid, it was an aggregate of disconnected sense-data, and had very little to say about the buildings or about the world for which they were intended."[33] The remark revealed the core of his concerns: architecture's social principles. Although the penguins were cute, Lubetkin insisted his intention was always "to build socialistically,"[34] and Moholy-Nagy's film had missed the point.

And so in 1935, when the revolution had supposedly arrived with Highpoint I, England had in fact already witnessed high modernist forms. Tecton's own Penguin Pool was one case, but Wells Coates' Lawn Road Flats (1934) in Belsize Park, London, not far from Highpoint I, predated Lubetkin's tower blocks and was perhaps even more explicitly concerned with building "socialistically" than anything Lubetkin had designed at that point (Figure 1.6).

Its flats reflected the spirit of *Existenzminimum* planning more than Highpoint I's upscale flowing spaces, and use of its communal areas was actively encouraged. Coates' concept was quite radical for an English context.

Figure 1.6 Lawn Road (Isokon) Flats, London. Photo: Leo Eigen.

The flats were small and utilitarian, and Jack Pritchard, who commissioned the structure, emphasized the communal aspect of the building, a rather non-English amenity, whereas the ground-floor common rooms at Highpoint I went unused.[35] Marcel Breuer, Hungarian and Jewish by birth and by 1935 an émigré in London, designed furniture for Pritchard's company, Isokon, as well as a ground-floor restaurant in the building – the Isobar – that served as a gathering spot for the residents who, in the thirties, included among others Gropius, Moholy-Nagy, Piet Mondrian, Henry Moore, and Agatha Christie, all at the same time, among other well-known intellectuals. Nevertheless, Lawn Road also offered flat-cleaning and room service from the restaurant; like Highpoint, it was part of a conscious attempt to link the possibility of flat-living with a somewhat luxurious lifestyle. Both tower blocks, then, were significant, and not just because they were visually conspicuous.[36] While the images of gleaming white structures rising from amidst the terraced brick houses in their neighborhoods are stunning and memorable, the white-walled exterior and international style aesthetic were known to the residents in those affluent areas. In the early thirties, the modern "look" was seen as "a sign of advanced good taste, a matter for intellectuals" and indicative of scientific efficiency.[37] Thus even more remarkable is the historical moment; that is, the buildings were realized in a time and place where the general ideal remained a private home and private garden, though Lubetkin considered the notion of *Gemütlichkeit* to be sheer nonsense.[38] In fact, flat-living was becoming increasingly widespread throughout Britain, even for upper social classes, and these structures were helping to legitimize the trend.[39]

And yet, there are important differences. In spite of its social intentions and clean lines, Lawn Road's forms felt heavier and more earthbound than Highpoint's. Lubetkin's structure is taller and more vertical; lifted up on *pilotis*, it was at the time emblematic of a modernist lightness. Ultimately, the buildings had related but different meanings. A quick scan of Highpoint I seems to lead directly to Le Corbusier's Five Points, among the most important of all architectural statements of the twentieth century, first published in 1926. The architectural principles put forth in the Five Points were rooted in the use of reinforced concrete, which allowed for a structure and its façade to exist as separate elements; the liberation of the façade from structural burdens enabled open interior spaces and walls with generous windows. The Five Points – delineated as *pilotis*, a roof garden, the free plan, the ribbon window, and the free façade – were the building blocks of "a fundamentally new aesthetic."[40] By raising a building on *pilotis*, Le Corbusier lightened the look of architecture, but also suggested buildings that looked toward an entire theory of city planning. Roadways could pass underneath buildings, and the lost ground-level space reappeared in the rooftop gardens that provided access to sunlight; these concepts were how he analyzed Highpoint I. Building tall meant structures could be spaced far apart, providing green areas and open air, even in a city. *Pilotis*, then, had important implications, suggesting an urban setting as well as new architectural forms for that metropolis. *Pilotis* implied tall skyscrapers, and tall skyscrapers implied a large, populated, urban community.[41]

The truth, though, was that Highpoint I's walls carried the weight, and the *pilotis* were not performing the structural role they suggested. These were not technically the Five Points; however, Lubetkin knew there was symbolism and social content inherent in the use of *pilotis*. Arup, Lubetkin's perpetually beleaguered engineer, explained:

> Lubetkin welcomed my proposal to do away with columns and beams, and then, typically, as I was to discover, proceeded to make it almost impossible for me to do so . . . That the block of flats had to be put on columns à la Corbusier was a purely architectural device. It would be difficult to pretend that it is useful in this case.[42]

Lubetkin never denied relying upon the theoretical implications of the *pilotis*, the so-called "symbolic essence" referred to by later scholarship, as opposed to the function offered by the *pilotis*. In his papers he warned against conceiving "design exclusively in terms of utility" and ignoring "architecture's symbolic language" as well as its "emotions,"[43] thus Moholy-Nagy's film about the Penguin Pool having enraged him. It ignored the social component of architecture, but furthermore, Lubetkin explicitly rejected empiricism and logical positivism – prevailing modes of analytical thought in thirties England and predicated exactly on the central importance of the sort of "sense-data" at the center of the film; i.e., a lack of interest in conceptual analysis.[44] Lubetkin's notes reflected on the "inability of direct observation to define the essence of . . . phenomena, [and] the inadequacy of sense perception" and criticized an "[i]nability to . . . find the truth behind the facts, to pass beyond the given form."[45] The insistence on *pilotis* and the reworkings of the structural system to accommodate them was integral to the "symbolic" functioning of Highpoint. Lubetkin is rarely discussed in terms of urbanism, but he knew that his use of *pilotis* would hint at Le Corbusier's search for new manifestations of city planning.[46] And so, the subsequent commissioning of Highpoint II on the adjacent site was an auspicious sign for modernist town planners and architects. The possibility of a companion tower block and a *Ville Radieuse* in the hills overlooking the congestion of central London, with its spreading roadways, must have been tantalizing. But to those who expected a continuation of early thirties ideals, Highpoint II's apparent yielding to façadism, flats that were even more luxurious than those in the first Highpoint, and no Radiant City were all disillusioning.

The sense that the two Highpoints stand for a larger, more generalized ebbing and flowing of modernist ideals is not without context for thirties Britain, as modern architecture had been slow to take hold once migrating from continental Europe. Henry-Russell Hitchcock traced its appearance in England, and was alert to the country's grappling with the new architecture as well as the struggle architects and builders faced as they came to terms with modernism on several different levels, trying to jettison historical styles but also to understand new building methods. A 1928 essay he wrote in *Cahiers d'Art* concluded optimistically: English modern architects would eventually "develop seriously, vigorously, and individually."[47] Hitchcock and Philip Johnson had all but omitted Britain from their canonical 1932 show *Modern Architecture: International Exhibition* at MoMA, including only Joseph Emberton's 1931 Royal Corinthian Yacht Club. The attention to Emberton indicates that the English modernist scene was little known, as only a year later, Emberton's colleagues in London singled him out and criticized him for not being modern enough. Hitchcock did not acknowledge the appearance of international style modernism in Britain until 1937, when he curated *Modern Architecture in England*, also for MoMA.

Just as Hitchcock had sensed that such architecture made its mark in fits and starts in England, competing incarnations of avant-garde modernists, sometime modernists, and anti-modernists were all part of the thirties mix, and assorted collectives came and went with varying levels of activity. The short-lived group Unit One was one attempt British modernists made to assert their presence, though it was active only from 1933 to 1935. An interdisciplinary group founded by the painter Paul Nash and championed by the art historian Herbert Read, who later was instrumental in the founding of London's ICA (Institute of Contemporary Arts), Unit One held one exhibition before unofficially disbanding. In 1937, *Circle: International Survey of Constructivist Art* was published in London (and featured work by English artists Barbara Hepworth and Henry Moore, as well as some of the most significant international artists and architects of the day, such as Le Corbusier, El Lissitzky, Constantin Brancusi, Richard Neutra, et al.), but plans for subsequent issues never materialized.

The year Highpoint II was completed, 1938, was in fact an active year for various vanguards to search for their bearings. The MARS (Modern Architectural Research) Group, the British offshoot of CIAM (Congrès Internationaux d'Architecture Moderne), was publicly chastised by a group of AA students for its "formalist escapism" and avoidance of political issues, having prepared an exhibition called *New Architecture* featuring work that was old by continental European standards.[48] MARS became increasingly important, especially in the forties, but its relationship to CIAM was at first tenuous, and from the start Lubetkin was skeptical; 1938 marked the final year he claimed membership. He questioned the Group's elusive use of "research" in the name and denounced its tendency to collaborate with established professional institutions. In his notebooks, he declared that his work was not self-expression nor intended for an elitist salon of MARS gentlemen,[49] "but a thesis . . . [and] social reflection."[50]

Also in 1938, Lubetkin and his Tecton colleagues went head to head against the Churchill government to oppose its policy on air raid precaution (ARP) shelters.[51] Under the auspices of the Architects' and Technicians' Organization (ATO), an organization that Lubetkin and others had founded in 1934 largely in opposition to MARS, Tecton proposed underground, communal bunkers in place of the official policy that advocated the use of existing basements, surface shelters, or prefabricated sheds each family could install in its garden (Figure 1.7).

Fueled by a general feeling among progressive intellectuals that England especially, but Europe too, needed a vocal, leftwing movement, the ATO "came together on a purely social and political basis," Lubetkin wrote.[52] Although the membership rolls of the two groups overlapped, the ATO identified concerns that foregrounded ideas before building. MARS might have expressed an affinity for modern forms and spouted claims about the intellectual act of research, but the ATO's language was aggressive and

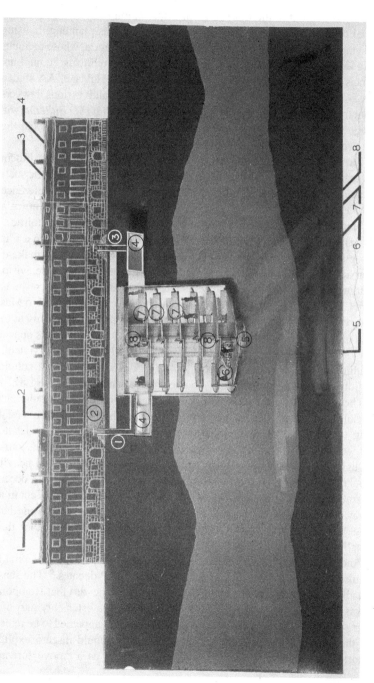

Figure 1.7 Design for a circular underground air raid shelter for Finsbury Borough Council, London. Used with permission from RIBApix.

angry, lashing out at the London architecture community for ignoring the social purpose of architecture.[53] Policy issues, such as planning, housing, and employment conditions, became the focus of the group, whose members included not only Lubetkin, but his fellow Tecton architects Samuel and Francis Skinner, the scientists J.D. Bernal and J.B.S. Haldane, AA student Cox – the one who later pilloried Highpoint II – and various lawyers, economists, and sociologists. The inaugural issue of the *ATO Bulletin*, with unsigned essays on architecture and housing filtered through Marxist theory, proclaimed outright: "We make no apologies."[54]

The ARP controversy into which Lubetkin and the ATO inserted themselves had been brewing for some time. Mass Observation, the prolific social science research group, reported that the increasingly common references to ARPs became "the outward symbols of what has now become known as the Home Front" and the term ARP was commonplace by the late thirties.[55] *William and A.R.P*, a children's book that was eventually made into a film, was published in 1939.[56] The ATO declared the government's make-do approach to bomb protection to be inadequate. Lubetkin went on television to argue the case for his specialized subterranean shelters, but a response from Churchill's secretary to Tecton's book *Planned ARP* indicated to Mass Observation that England's extreme detachment from the collectivity at the heart of modern architecture elsewhere was part of the government's opposition to Tecton's bunkers, and as Lubetkin historians Peter Coe and Malcolm Reading have discerned, the opposition also pointed to a general cultural hostility toward large populations amassed in urban centers (Figure 1.8).[57]

The discussion of bomb shelters, of course, reflects particular and extraordinary circumstances, but in it, we catch a glimpse of Tecton's totalizing vision. The ARP issue also prefigures and illuminates the debates that would continue to surround English and European planning discourse through the period of reconstruction, when those who advocated heavily populated cities opposed those who favored regional dispersal and decentralization. ARPs, and the ATO more generally, functioned for Tecton as a way to inject into architecture the research component (and strong language) that Lubetkin saw MARS talking around and about, rather than actually tackling.

And yet, the importance of the short-lived ATO has at times been quickly dismissed as it faded out in the aftermath of the ARP debates.[58] The sense that all this action had been in vain perhaps supports the idea that Highpoint II was part of a step back. Although Highpoint I was ostensibly part of a larger architectural and social revolution, Highpoint II appeared to be rejecting the basic modernist premise that architecture should discard explicit historical references. In seeing the second building as a "move forward

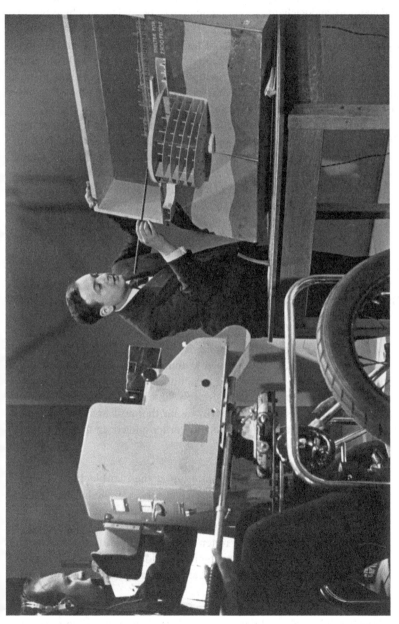

Figure 1.8 Berthold Lubetkin on television discussing ARPs. © BBC. Used with permission.

from functionalism," Richards commended it as "more human" than the first Highpoint he had eagerly embraced. Three years had passed, concerns had changed, and Richards was content to leave behind the machine-purism of heroic age modernism. Highpoint II was a reprieve, somehow seeming as approachable as the cozy details of his New Empiricism. Richards drew upon endemic strains of empirical thought to make his case, and Highpoint II satisfied his increased focus on architecture's relationship to "the man in the street," the abstractions of the international style having grown illegible and inexpressive to all but a specialized few.[59]

The idea of focusing on "the common man" that was cultivated and debated throughout Europe in the postwar years actually appeared in England in the early thirties, when there were rumblings within the London avant-garde community that the readability of artistic forms needed to matter. In 1931, for instance, the aforementioned art historian Herbert Read had presented an argument for abstract art but asserted that such "elite" art could not stand on its own; the book in which his argument appears is called *The Meaning of Art: An Introduction for the Plain Man*.[60] In 1933, the architect Frederic Towndrow wrote a book called *Architecture in the Balance: An Approach to the Art of Scientific Humanism*, which maintained that architecture must appeal to a sense of commonality among individuals.[61] By 1940, the overriding concern of the MARS Group was unmistakable: "Modern architecture must come to terms with ordinary people."[62]

Highpoint II, then, seems to make cultural sense. Of course, such a view assumes that the classical caryatids were in fact legible to the man in the street, which Richards seemed to think, and it also ignores everything Lubetkin seems to have stood for. Publicly Lubetkin was an activist, and privately he championed architecture's "intellectual character," railing against whimsical design.[63] Cox's was by far the most notorious reaction to Highpoint II, a part of which has been earlier quoted. In the AA journal *Focus* he further wrote:

> Standing in the garden and looking up at the two blocks, 1935 and 1938, it is clear that something has changed . . . [O]ne has the feeling that a *form* has been imposed . . . The intellectual approach which has produced what we know as modern architecture is fundamentally a functionalist approach . . . a rotten name for the antithesis of formalism, because it carries with it dehumanised ideas which nobody wishes to defend . . . [m]y contention is that the recent work of Tecton shows a deviation from this approach.[64]

Highpoint II, Cox felt, had devolved into formalism, impossible to square with the ATO's protest mentality. The brazen addition of the caryatids was an obvious offense, but more seriously, Lubetkin's architecture no longer seemed to mark the road ahead to a new social order. Cox's message is clear: Lubetkin had chosen decorative aesthetics (far different from the symbolism of Highpoint I's *pilotis*) over social and functional obligations.

Reyner Banham, however, tersely dismissed both of these arguments at once. Lubetkin, he wrote, is "the distinguished Russian refugee whose political convictions had never led him to compromise with vernacular standards."[65] He left his contentions unexplained, but is Highpoint II, as Banham suggested, neither the comfort Richards sought nor the disastrous renunciation of socialist ideals Cox found?

Notes

1 *OED* (*Oxford English Dictionary*) (1989), s.v. "tectonic."
2 Christina Lodder, *Russian Constructivism* (New Haven and London: Yale University Press, 1983), 94 and 99.
3 Stanford Anderson, "Modern Architecture and Industry: Peter Behrens, the AEG, and Industrial Design," *Oppositions* 21 (Summer 1980): 83. Kenneth Frampton quotes this as well in "Towards a Critical Regionalism: Six Points for an Architecture of Resistance," in Hal Foster, ed., *The Anti-Aesthetic: Essays on Postmodern Culture* (Port Townsend, WA: The Bay Press, 1983), 27–8. Anderson is summarizing the definition offered by Karl Bötticher, a German aesthetician who defined the concept in 1852. For a broader discussion, see Frampton, *Studies in Tectonic Culture* (Cambridge, MA: The MIT Press, 1995).
4 John Allan, *Berthold Lubetkin: Architecture and the Tradition of Progress* (London: RIBA, 1992), 110. This indispensable book remains the most exhaustive and complete source on Lubetkin to date. Other useful and general works include Peter Coe and Malcolm Reading, *Lubetkin and Tecton: Architecture and Social Commitment* (London: The Arts Council of Great Britain, 1981) and Reading and Coe, *Lubetkin & Tecton: An Architectural Study* (London: Triangle Architectural Publishing, 1992). A more recent work by Allan is a book of photographs of Lubetkin buildings; Allan, *Berthold Lubetkin* (London: Merrell, 2002). All subsequent Allan footnotes refer to his 1992 book. For discussion of the history of the AA see John Summerson, "How We Began: The Early History of the Architectural Association," *The Architect and Building News* (April 25, 1947): 74–9 or more recently, Alan Powers, ed., *H.S. Goodhart-Rendel 1887–1959* (London: The Architectural Association, 1987).
5 Joan Ockman has suggested that the "bureaucratic," teamwork-oriented model for architectural production was a norm in the postwar world, but certainly not in the thirties. See Ockman, "Toward a Theory of Normative Architecture," in Steven Harris and Deborah Berke, eds., *Architecture of the Everyday* (New York: Princeton Architectural Press, 1997), 131–5. The vagaries of the alliances within Tecton, the drifting in and out of the firm of various partners and employees, and the firm's eventual dissolution in the forties (with some ill-will remaining between Lubetkin and Denys Lasdun, a later member of the firm) is outside the scope of this book. For our purposes here, the firm's work and Lubetkin's work will be considered synonymous. For a detailed, biography-oriented recounting of the changes in the firm throughout Lubetkin's career, see Allan, *Lubetkin*.

6   The Gestetner family was based in north London; their company manufactured office equipment. In the late twenties, the family had commissioned the industrial designer Raymond Loewy to redesign their copy machine. Both Highpoint structures have been extensively described in the existing literature, so my descriptions of the buildings will be fairly general and will refer to others' reports on the visual elements. For example, see the aforementioned works by Allan, and Coe and Reading. Also see William Curtis, *English Architecture 1930s: The Modern Movement in England 1930–9* (Milton Keynes: The Open University Press, 1975); Reading, "Tall Order," *The Architects' Journal* 181 (June 5, 1985): 44–56; Thomas Diehl, "Theory and Principle: Berthold Lubetkin's Highpoint One and Highpoint Two," *Journal of Architectural Education* 4 (May 1999): 233–41.

7   Allan, *Lubetkin*, 277. Ove Arup later explained that the windows caused all sorts of engineering issues – the large openings "cut away most of the wall . . . leaving only wall strips on each side to take the vertical load" in Arup, "The Engineer Looks Back: Arup Associations," *AR 30s*, special issue of *The Architectural Review* 166 (November 1979): 316. Arup discusses the entire construction in that same memoir, pp. 315–21.

8   Quoted by Reyner Banham, *Theory and Design in the First Machine Age* (Cambridge, MA: The MIT Press, 1960), 324.

9   Gallery access tended to be a more economical means of organization and had been thought to provide better ventilation in the flats, but because blocks of flats had originally been considered a lower-class form of public housing, gallery access was also a means of insuring that tenants could be more easily supervised by the authorities, and by the thirties, it was associated with "dirty people." See Miles Glendinning and Stefan Muthesius, *Tower Block: Modern Public Housing in England, Scotland, Wales and Northern Ireland* (New Haven and London: The Paul Mellon Centre for Studies in British Art and Yale University Press, 1994), 69. The importance of this book as a resource cannot be underestimated.

10 Coe and Reading, *Lubetkin and Tecton*, 122.

11 Berthold Lubetkin, "Flats in Rosebery Avenue, Finsbury," *The Architectural Review* 109 (March 1951): 140. The essay as a whole (pp. 138–50) consists of Lubetkin's own descriptions of the structural systems used in both Highpoints, his 1935 Cement Marketing Company competition entry, and other Tecton projects.

12 Allan, *Lubetkin*, 53.

13 Anthony Cox, "Highpoint II, North Hill, Highgate," *Focus* 2 (Winter 1948): 71–9.

14 Curtis, *English Architecture*, 52; John Summerson, "The MARS Group and the Thirties," in John Bold and Edward Chaney, eds., *English Architecture, Public and Private* (London: The Hambledon Press, 1993), 303–10, and Summerson, introductory essay to Trevor Dannatt, *Modern Architecture in Britain* (London: Arts Council of Great Britain, 1959), 17.

15 Some canonical essays include Eric de Maré, "The New Empiricism: The Antecedents and Origins of Sweden's Latest Style," *The Architectural Review* 103 (January 1948): 9–10; Ivor de Wolfe, "Townscape: A Plea for English Visual Philosophy Founded on the True Rock of Sir Uvedale Price," *The Architectural Review* 106 (December 1949): 355–62. Michela Rosso has studied *The Architectural Review* in detail. See Rosso, *La storia utile: Patrimonio e modernità nel lavoro di John Summerson e Nikolaus Pevsner: Londra 1928–1955* (Torino: Edizioni di Comunità, 2001).

16 Banham quoting A. Smithson in "The New Brutalism," *The Architectural Review* 118 (December 1955): 356.

17 Louise Campbell, *Coventry Cathedral: Art and Architecture in Post-war Britain* (Oxford: Oxford University Press, 1996), 261.

18 Cox, "Highpoint II," 79.

19 Richards, "Highpoint Number Two," 166.

20 Le Corbusier, "The Vertical Garden City," 9.

21 Clough Williams-Ellis, *England and the Octopus* (Portmeirion: Penrhyndeudraeth, 1928 [1975]), 62.

22 Le Corbusier, "Vertical Garden City," 9–10.

23 Kenneth Frampton, *Modern Architecture: A Critical History* (London: Thames & Hudson, 1992), 180.

24 "Penguin Pond," *Architectural Record* 77 (February 1935): 107. "Bassin des pingouins dans le zoo de Londres," *L'architecture d'aujourd'hui* 5 (September 1934): 60–2. Hadas A. Steiner places the Penguin Pool within a larger discussion of modern architecture and picturesque theory in England in "For the Birds," *Grey Room* 13 (Fall 2003): 5–31.

25 Curtis, *English Architecture 1930s*, 52; Manfredo Tafuri and Francesco Dal Co, *Modern Architecture* vol. 2, trans. Robert Erich Wolf (London: Faber & Faber, 1980 [1976]), 257–9.

26 Allan, *Lubetkin*, 19–39.

27 Many of Lubetkin's notes on Russian Constructivism are located in his private papers, held by the British Architectural Library of the Royal Institute of British Architects (RIBA). Archival folders hereafter referred to by the abbreviation RIBA followed by the folder number. RIBA LuB/20/4 contains notes from the sixties on the importance of the Russian Revolution on the development of modern art; RIBA LuB/20/5 contains an unpublished draft (c. 1962) of a book on Soviet architecture.

28 Allan, *Lubetkin*, 133. See Lodder, *Russian Constructivism*, 12 and 269n.32; Catherine Cooke, *Russian Avant-Garde: Theories of Art, Architecture, and the City* (London: Academy Editions, 1995), 146; Camilla Gray, *The Great Experiment: Russian Art 1863–1922* (London: Thames & Hudson, 1962), 215–18, 309n.7. Cooke calls Lubetkin an important post-revolutionary link between Russia and Europe.

29 Berthold Lubetkin, "Architectural Thought since the Revolution," and "Recent Developments of Town Planning in U.S.S.R.," *The Architectural Review* 71 (May 1932): 201–3 (part 1) and 209–14 (part 2).

30 Lubetkin, "Architectural Thought since the Revolution," 202. Allan has discussed the curve as a motif in Lubetkin's work; see Allan, *Lubetkin*, 209. In addition to the Highpoints, large, circular sculptural forms appear often in Lubetkin's work; see for example, Whipsnade (bungalows, 1933–6; zoo, 1934–5); the grand stairway at Bevin Court (1954) in Holford Square, London; the landscape design and library in the Dorset Estate, London (1951–7).

31 Terence A. Senter, "Moholy-Nagy in England" (MPhil thesis, University of Nottingham, 1977), chapter 3.

32 Senter, "Moholy-Nagy in England," 102–3.

33 Senter, "Moholy-Nagy in England," 166.

34 Lubetkin, "Architectural Thought since the Revolution," 201. Also quoted in Anthony Jackson, *The Politics of Architecture: A History of Modern Architecture in Britain* (London: The Architectural Press, 1970), 44 and in Curtis, *English Architecture 1930s*, 51.

35 Pritchard is a fascinating figure who deserves more study. See his memoir *View from a Long Chair* (Boston and London: Routledge and Kegan Paul, 1984). He had been instrumental in helping Gropius and Moholy-Nagy acquire work in London, and he had also hired Le Corbusier and Moholy-Nagy to design exhibition stands for his Venesta Plywood Company. See "Modern Flats at Hampstead," *The Architectural Review* 76 (July 1934): 77–82, for a feature on Lawn Road.

36 Allan notes that it was Lubetkin's great sadness that Highpoint I's communal spaces were largely unused (Allan, *Lubetkin*, 280). Lubetkin's attitude toward the communal areas was inspired by Ginzburg.

37 Glendinning and Muthesius, *Tower Block*, 12.

38 Glendinning and Muthesius, *Tower Block*, 95.

39 On the increasing importance of flats, see F.R.S. Yorke and Frederick Gibberd, *The Modern Flat* (London: The Architectural Press, 1937) and Elizabeth Denby, *Europe Re-housed* (London: George Allen & Unwin Ltd., 1938). For a historical and social discussion, see Glendinning and Muthesius, *Tower Block*. Conspicuous though the Lawn Road Flats block was, as an absolutely fascinating side note, the landscape and siting of the structure allowed residents to come and go essentially unobserved. This unintentionally allowed the building to be used as a home by Soviet spies working on covert operations against Britain during the thirties and into the Cold War. See David Burke, *The Lawn Road Flats: Spies, Writers, and Artists* (Woodbridge, UK and Rochester, NY: The Boydell Press, 2014) and Burke, "The Lawn Road Flats," *The Spy Who Came in from the Co-op: Melita Norwood and the Ending of Cold War Espionage* (Woodbridge: The Boydell Press, 2008), 71–83.

40 Le Corbusier and Pierre Jeanneret, "Five Points toward a New Architecture," reprinted in Ulrich Conrads, ed., trans. Michael Bullock, *Programs and Manifestoes on Twentieth-Century Architecture* (Cambridge, MA: The MIT Press, 1970), 99–101.

41 Muthesius and Glendinning write that "For the Smithsons, the *pilotis* of Le Corbusier's [*Unité*] were 'symbols of the participation of the *Unité* in the life of Marseilles'" (*Tower Block*, 116). Later, though, in the early seventies, Peter Smithson threw Le Corbusier's terminology back at him and rejected the proposition that a "vertical garden city" in the manner of the *Unité* at all countered the problems of the "horizontal" garden city. Smithson claimed that horizontal garden cities and the last two *Unités* that Corbusier built (Briey-en-Forêt, 1957–63 and Firminy-Vert, 1956–70) all suffered from an air of isolation, poor local shopping, long commutes to work, a too-low population density, etc., that had drained the "cities" of any "sense of connection" (Peter Smithson, "Toulouse le Mirail," *Architectural Design* 41 [October 1971]: 599–601).

42 Arup, "The Engineer Looks Back," 316.

43 RIBA LuB/17/2. On modern architecture's symbolism, see William Jordy, "The Symbolic Essence of Modern European Architecture of the Twenties and its Continuing Influence," *Journal of the Society of Architectural Historians* 22 (1963): 177–87.

44 A.J. Ayer, *Language, Truth and Logic* (New York: Dover Publications, Inc., 1946 [1936]) and *The Foundations of Empirical Knowledge* (London: Macmillan & Co., 1940). For an analysis of the way Ayer was used in discussions of art and to counter abstraction, see Anne Massey, *The Independent Group: Modernism and Mass Culture in Britain, 1945–59* (Manchester and New York: Manchester University Press, 1995), chapter 1. Peter Galison suggests that empiricism can

nonetheless be theory-laden, in Galison, "Aufbau/Bauhaus: Logical Positivism and Architectural Modernism," *Critical Inquiry* 16 no. 4 (Summer 1990): 752n.82.

45 RIBA LuB/17/3. Some of Lubetkin's notes are undated, but these quotations seem to be from the 1980s, as Lubetkin mused on art and culture. Curtis also wrote of the tendency toward empiricism in the interwar period, identifying that one "of the most striking features of the climate of modern architectural criticism of the thirties in England was the blindness to symbolic and fantasy qualities of modern architecture, the tendency to accept functionalist explanations at face value," in Curtis, "Berthold Lubetkin, or 'Socialist' Architect in the Diaspora," *Architectural Association Quarterly (AAQ)* 8 (1976): 39n.6.

46 A failed attempt to design a master plan for the New Town of Peterlee (1948–50) was his only foray into full-fledged town planning, although he had been offered the chance to design Stevenage New Town, a proposal he rejected. Coe and Reading have written that "Lubetkin and Tecton never developed a codified theory of urban planning or mass housing," in their *Lubetkin and Tecton*, 139. There is very little published about Peterlee; even at the time, the Master Plan for the scheme was not published in the architectural press, though it did receive some coverage. General sources include Allan, *Lubetkin*, 448–518. A short essay by Monica Felton, Chairman of the Peterlee Development Corporation, is useful; see "Britain's Model New Industrial Town: Peterlee," *Journal of the American Institute of Planners* 15 no. 1 (Spring 1949): 40–3.

47 Henry-Russell Hitchcock, "L'Architecture Contemporaine en Angleterre," *Cahiers d'Art* (1928): 446. Translation mine.

48 "The MARS Exhibition." Reviewed by students in Unit 15 of the AA School. *Architectural Association Journal* 53 (February 1938): 386–8.

49 RIBA LuB/19/1 (letter to Wells Coates dated January 10, 1933). The letter is also reprinted in *AR 30s*, special issue of *The Architectural Review* 166 (November 1979): 330.

50 RIBA LuB/17/7.

51 See, for instance, RIBA LuB/3; AASTA, *A.R.P.: A Report on the Design, Equipment and Cost of Air-Raid Shelters* (London: The Architects' Journal, 1938). Includes foreword by the ARP Committee and a reprint of a related article from *The Architects' Journal* (July 7, 1938); J.B.S. Haldane, *A.R.P.* (London: Victor Gollancz, 1938); Haldane, *How to be Safe from Air Raids* (London: Victor Gollancz, 1938); commentary on a speech given by Haldane in 1938 at a RIBA conference devoted to the ARP debate, "A.R.P.: The Informal Meeting on 14 December," *Journal of the Royal Institute of British Architects* 46 (January 9, 1939): 238; Felix Samuely, "Aspects of A.R.P.," *Focus* 3 (Spring 1939): 48–52; Haldane, "The Mathematics of Air Raid Protection," *Journal of the Royal Institute of British Architects* 46 (January 9, 1939): 240–1. For general overviews, see Allan, *Lubetkin*, 352–63; Coe and Reading, *Lubetkin and Tecton*, 162–8; and Andrew Saint, *Towards a Social Architecture: The Role of School Building in Post-War England* (New Haven and London: Yale University Press, 1987), 12.

52 Lubetkin, "Modern Architecture in England," *American Architect and Architecture* 150 (February 1937): 30.

53 RIBA SaG/90/2.

54 *ATO Bulletin* 1 (May 1936) unpaginated, filed in RIBA SaG/90/1. The *Bulletin* is a small pamphlet, only a handful of pages, even though the editorial statement announcing the first issue considered it a full-fledged "new architectural magazine" that would be published bi-monthly. Only two issues were produced.

55 Tom Harrisson and Charles Madge, eds., *War Begins at Home* (London: Chatto & Windus/Mass Observation, 1940), 5.

56 Richmal Crompton, *William and A.R.P.* (London: George Newnes, 1939). Crompton's *William* publications, about a mischievous young boy, were a popular series of children's books from the twenties to the forties.

57 Coe and Reading, *Lubetkin and Tecton*, 167–8.

58 On the short-lived avant-garde collectives in thirties Britain, see David Dean, *The Thirties: Recalling the English Architectural Scene* (London: Trefoil Books, 1983), 113. On the fading out of the ATO, see Allan, *Lubetkin*, 329–30.

59 Untitled piece, credited to James MacQuedy, Richards's pseudonym, *The Architectural Review* 87 (May 1940): 183–4; Richards, "Architecture and the Common Man," *The Architects' Journal* 107 (February 5, 1948): 132–3. The man in the street is discussed throughout the MARS papers deposited in Ernö Goldfinger's files, RIBA GoEr/310/4. For a general discussion see Eric Mumford, *The CIAM Discourse on Urbanism, 1928–1960* (Cambridge, MA: The MIT Press, 2000), 163–79.

60 Herbert Read, *The Meaning of Art* (London: Faber & Faber, 1931). The American edition was called *Anatomy of Art* (New York: Dodd, Mead & Company, 1932).

61 Frederic Towndrow, *Architecture in the Balance: An Approach to the Art of Scientific Humanism* (London: Chatto & Windus, 1933).

62 RIBA GoEr/310/4.

63 RIBA LuB/17/3. Allan notes that at the time, Lubetkin was touting the caryatids as mere garden ornaments; if taken at face value, this is remarkable, for Lubetkin's sense that they could be considered separate from the building itself. Tecton architect Anthony Chitty did view the caryatids as "a piece of whimsy," in Allan, *Lubetkin*, 298.

64 Cox, "Highpoint II, North Hill, Highgate," 71–9. The review is also quoted in Curtis, *English Architecture 1930s*, 70; Frampton, *Modern Architecture*, 252; Jackson, *Politics of Architecture*, 47–8. Emphasis original.

65 Reyner Banham, *The New Brutalism: Ethic or Aesthetic* (New York: Reinhold Publishing Corporation, 1966), 14.

2 London calling

High stakes, high relief

Classical caryatids aside for a moment, the close connections between Highpoints I and II remain important. The buildings were meant to flow together visually, and they offer each other a context through the alignment of their windows and in the similarity of Highpoint II's wings to the bulk of Highpoint I, "to preserve unity," wrote Lubetkin.[1] The buildings half-share a structural technique and similar cladding in places, but fully share crucial modernist elements such as rooftop gardens, *portes-cochères* designed for cars, and ribbon windows, and, in spite of the caryatids, modernist *pilotis* do in fact dominate much of the overall exterior of both buildings. Along with his extremely in-depth studies of the two buildings, John Allan, Lubetkin's biographer, has also emphasized with great detail the fact that the structures are only six feet apart. Clearly Highpoints I and II are meant to interact, and to an extent, their similarities are meant to highlight their differences, and vice versa.

The international style in thirties England was a loaded cultural fact that cannot be divorced from the two Highpoints. On the one hand, its presence can be placed fairly simply within a larger history of the dissemination of modern architecture; this journey and its arrival in England are what interested Hitchcock. But on the other hand, its incidence in England was far from simple.[2] Perhaps MARS avoided bold declarations while the ATO thrived on them, but the international style unto itself was politically laden in England, in spite of any intentions (or not) on the part of its architects. Whitewashed walls might have started to pop up and be recognized as modern, but that does not mean they did not carry with them some controversy. The sense of modern forms as foreign intrusions upon native soil was of course not a new construct or prejudice; the 1927 Weissenhofsiedlung, where international style architecture became a codified aesthetic and its concomitant goal of providing standardized housing prototypes truly coalesced, was famously derided as an Arab village. Such derision was a real presence, and as soon as modern architecture came face to face with

English ideologies, an awareness of its foreignness and what that meant in various circles was widespread. For many, international modern forms were destroying British culture in spite of a general understanding that such forms were meant to be universally adaptable; the Scottish planner Patrick Abercrombie, for instance, was called "un-British" for his interest in modernist planning. Reginald Blomfield's 1934 book *Modernismus*, a British version of a "blood and soil" treatise in the manner of Paul Schultze-Naumburg, attacked French and German modernism, though really it was a larger statement against both the growing presence of foreigners in England and internationalism as an artistic ideal.[3] That same year Blomfield challenged modern architect and MARS member Amyas Connell to an on-air BBC radio debate entitled "For and Against Modern Architecture," in which he focused on the international style's foreignness.

That discussion of these forms and endeavors revolved around their foreignness is not unexpected in a culture that George Orwell had described more largely as narrow-minded and anti-foreign.[4] Some had addressed the situation with humor, such as Evelyn Waugh's portrayal of the architect Otto Silenus in *Decline and Fall* (1928), written just as modern architecture was starting to permeate England, but to others, the increasing visibility of foreigners and a lack of attention to nationalism in the arts were insidious. A nationalistic discourse of Englishness in the arts was deep-rooted, long before Pevsner sought to explain and understand it, and modern architecture was at odds with it.[5] Often, the rejection of modernism was explicitly laid out in anti-Semitic terms, whether or not the architects were Jewish. Foreigners and Jews were lumped together as outsiders. A letter published in a 1935 issue of *The Architects' Journal* by a young British architect named Keith Aitken warned readers "we must be on our guard against too readily drinking in Jewish-Communist doctrine, even when it is disguised in the most seductive of concrete and glass clothes."[6] Aitken's letter was in reference to the architect Chermayeff, linking him to a "Jewish tragedy" – not the persecution of Jews by others, but what Aitken saw as the unfailing ability of Jews to arouse antagonism.

As World War II approached, foreignness took on a new urgency. No longer merely synonymous with immigration or the shape of a roof, foreignness became inextricably tied to the plight of those who had to flee Nazi Germany. Whatever resistance might have been lurking, England nonetheless opened itself up and became known as a safe corner of Europe, the influx of refugees becoming a part of everyday culture.[7] London called to the refugees and freedom beckoned. England was seen as the center of the free world, with the BBC as its voice.[8] Within art and architectural history, the discussion surrounding England's reception of émigré artists and architects generally supports that impression. Read, for instance, described England in the thirties as a "nest of gentle artists" embracing foreigners entering the country, John Willett wrote that the émigré architects in London encountered little resistance because modern architecture was meant to be international in conception, and Dennis Sharp described the thirties in England as "polite," a mood he explicitly connected to the presence of the émigrés.[9]

Although gentle nests and politeness are reassuring, such refinement neglects to consider why there was a need for such good manners in the first place, glossing over the increasingly precarious situation on the continent and somewhat boorishly suggesting that all was fine simply because modern architecture was meant to be international anyway. In fact, the idea of politeness, in the context of British anti-Semitism, actually renders the situation more dire. In the early twentieth century in England, "Jewish identity was acceptable if Jews were committed to assimilation – to not being too 'loud' about their Jewishness."[10] Jews simply had to be quiet and blend in or risk discrimination. Even among intellectuals, anti-Semitic rhetoric was pervasive; H.G. Wells described Jews as "vulgar" in 1902, and the biases were ingrained enough by the middle of the century for Orwell to dissect British anti-Semitism in a 1945 essay.[11] The etiquette and politesse, then, were masking something deep, dark, and urgent. A forced ideology of assimilation, of not disrupting proper English society, was the cover for a seething anti-Semitism below the surface. To be polite and unobtrusive was, therefore, a political maneuver and cover-up operation. In her essay "The 'École Française' vs. the 'École de Paris': The Debate about the Status of Jewish Artists in Paris between the Wars," Romy Golan has shown that the term "École de Paris" was a neologism coined to distinguish Jewish artists from their "purer" French counterparts; Janet Wolff has shown that a similar differentiation occurred in England.[12] In her work on R.B. Kitaj, Wolff suggests that although there was no separate name for foreign or Jewish architects and artists, as there was in France, there was an institutionalized, officially sanctioned differentiation between Jewish-England and English-England. We will subsequently return to these ideas.

The exigency surrounding the resettlement of refugee architects has been well documented,[13] and although the RIBA set up a dedicated Refugee Committee to discuss how to handle the inundation of qualified professional architects, nonetheless the foreigners were called "problems," and issues of nationalism and citizenship forced a "conflict of loyalties."[14] This is hardly a gentle nest. The foreign architects were at the mercy of a slew of regulations, guidelines, and the hit-or-miss generosity of established figures or other foreigners who had already installed themselves in Britain. As was previously mentioned, refugee architects had to collaborate with those who were by this time registered in England, so in addition to the

Chermayeff/Mendelsohn partnership, scores of other connections were imposed. Gropius was taken in by Maxwell Fry, for instance, Marcel Breuer by F.R.S. Yorke, and Eugen Kaufmann by Frederic Towndrow. The partnerships produced real and significant work. Consider, for instance, the De La Warr Pavilion in Bexhill-on-Sea by Chermayeff and Mendelsohn (1935), or the Impington Village College buildings (1938–9) by Gropius and Fry, which are now listed buildings and considered emblematic of thirties modernism in England. And yet, in spite of the institutionalization of a system of collaboration, the fear of deportation was so strong among foreign architects that they often were afraid to be associated with, or vouch for the expertise of, other émigrés and colleagues, and historians have even identified widespread anti-Jewish sentiment present among British Jews themselves, especially during the interwar period.[15] The stakes were high, and the overall roster of interned intellectuals is massive. What must the then-converted Pevsner have been thinking when, in 1940, he received word of the death of his father, born Hillel Pewsner, his funeral held in Leipzig's only synagogue that survived Kristallnacht, followed by a traditional Jewish burial?[16]

Foreigners remained branded as such, or at least conscious of their difference, long after their initial entry to Britain, even though some, including Lubetkin as we have mentioned, had chosen to become émigrés years before they might have been forced into exile. Lubetkin's ancestors had faced pogroms in Tsarist Russia; thus, a voluntary émigré or not, once face to face with what was deeply embedded in England, how could his foreignness not matter?[17] Furthermore, architects who were non-British subjects were bound to rules of RIBA membership different from those of British subjects, criteria that kept them not only separate from their host country but from the profession in which they were experts as well.

Fry felt that the presence of the refugees gave the architectural community a morale boost and encouraged progressive thinking,[18] while Lubetkin believed (or at least proclaimed) otherwise. He wrote that the foreigners had little effect on the development of modern architecture in England, as continental ideals simply became meaningless in their new English "sociological conditions."[19] Ernst Gombrich, himself a Jew who fled Austria in 1939, rejected the idea of a refugee community at all. Gombrich criticized the reductive sense that all refugees necessarily shared a connection, although Antony Godfrey clearly identifies a close-knit and active German Jewish community in the Belsize Park area of London, one that worked collectively to transport their particular religious traditions to their new location.[20] The Mendelsohns and the Goldfingers all in fact lived in Highpoint I for a time, and somewhat touchingly, Eric Mendelsohn's daughter Esther babysat the Goldfinger children. Although that might not be the sort of community to which Gombrich referred, the issue was clearly important enough to debate.

In either case, whether the foreign architects were "good" for Britain and its architecture or not, what is notable is the generalized and continued linking of "not-English" and "modern." In fact, into the forties, "foreign" was used to spread anti-modernist propaganda, not simply within professional planning circles. In 1942, the RIBA sponsored an exhibition called *The Rebuilding of Britain*, meant to explain the damage the country had incurred during the war and what might be proposed in various reconstruction schemes. The catalogue cautioned that

> England after the war must be England, and not a schematically planned and blue-printed Utopia. By all means distrust the planner who promises an England gleamingly and glitteringly streamlined. We have a right to our countryside, our old towns, and our rhythm of life, different from anywhere else, and we have a right to our old brand of imperfections.[21]

The warning is sinister and xenophobic: streamlined modernist utopias were absolutely not English, and non-Englishness was by default suspect. In its English setting, according to the RIBA publication, the international style was automatically utopian and foreign, a nationalist cry incited by an architecture exhibition. In essence, the catalogue text was a call for picturesque planning, seen as a homegrown, English aesthetic that celebrated the seemingly rustic, casual, unplanned joy and surprise of non-classical gardens and rambling small towns. The admonition, though, was disingenuous, as the picturesque and its quaintness were as planned and artificially constructed as anything streamlined and modernist – designed, sham ruins are of course a cornerstone of picturesque landscapes – but the RIBA's language implied otherwise. Thus, if a rejection of the international style's gleaming and glittering "streamlinedness" was seen as a rejection of the foreign and therefore of the refugees, is Highpoint II's watered-down international style a return to old England, filtered through and coupled with such xenophobia? If so, then Highpoint II is far from the innocent calm or solace Richards thought he had found, and complicates the aims of Lubetkin, himself foreign.

Political links, though, were remote from Richards's impulse, whereas Cox indeed sought to make sure Lubetkin's architecture retained the social dimension of the earlier work. Cox was after something far-reaching, but so was Lubetkin, which is why it is inadequate to write off the caryatids merely in terms of shock or ambiguity or humor.[22] In fact, the whole of Highpoint II's design process has about it a profoundly subversive air. Highpoint I was noticed, and in its aftermath, an official planning committee instituted a series of height regulations, leaving no doubt that the local response to Highpoint I had been negative. Le Corbusier commented on the limitations, calling them "heartbreaking,"[23] and considering that the importance of height had become an integral part of the modernist polemic on housing, such legislation was not inconsequential. England's modernist planners and thinkers such as Goldfinger borrowed freely from Gropius's *The New Architecture and the Bauhaus* (1935) and circulated the idea that building taller would maximize daylight provisions.[24] In addition to answering to height restrictions, the preliminary schemes for Highpoint II were policed for overtly modernist forms in order to protect the character of the Highgate community and ensure that Highpoint I was not replicated. Lubetkin managed to undermine the watchful eye of planning authorities by submitting and resubmitting proposals and drawings in which modernist elements were concealed by pastiche, historical details (Figure 2.1). Drawings of Gothic arches, spires, and parapets masked a flat roof and ribbon windows. After the designs were approved and construction commenced, Lubetkin gradually eliminated much of the surface ornamentation to realize a more stripped-down structure. Nonetheless, Highpoint II remains less stripped-down than Highpoint I. Drawing attention to the brick, tile, balconies, stair towers, and other elements, Allan refers to a "bas-relief in the surface depth of the building" and the many "visual effects" that set it apart from the more monolithic solidity of Highpoint I (Figure 2.2).[25]

There is an international context for some of these aesthetic shifts; e.g., in 1935, Le Corbusier's Petite Maison de Weekend in La Celle-St.-Cloud embraced rough stone materials and archaic building techniques, and a pan-European turn toward surrealism in art brought with it a disdain for rationalism and an interest in Jungian myths and the deep, dark corners of the human psyche. There is, also, an enormous amount of homegrown justification for these "effects" as well; English architects too felt the impact of surrealist art, and experimentation with color also began to permeate modern architectural work and research in England.[26] Breuer's thirties plywood chairs, a move away from the tubular steel he used at the Bauhaus, were designed in London and reflect his patron Jack Pritchard's interest in the work of Alvar Aalto's "humanist" modernism. Goldfinger's 1938 house on Willow Road in London, designed for himself and his family, also used earthy brick and warm wooden detailing. But it has been too easy to dismiss Lubetkin's "less *sachlich*" moment as evidence of the failure of British modernism, instead of a strong decision on the part of Lubetkin to take a particular stance, a concession that is granted to other European modernisms as they gradually distanced themselves from hard-edged rationalism.[27]

A series of sketches Lubetkin executed as he designed Highpoint II indicate he wanted the caryatids to appear as if they resulted from a rational design choice – no supports looked too light, concrete *pilotis* looked too heavy, and the caryatids seemed just right – but coming from an avowed Marxist who linked his politics to his architecture, he was of course choosing

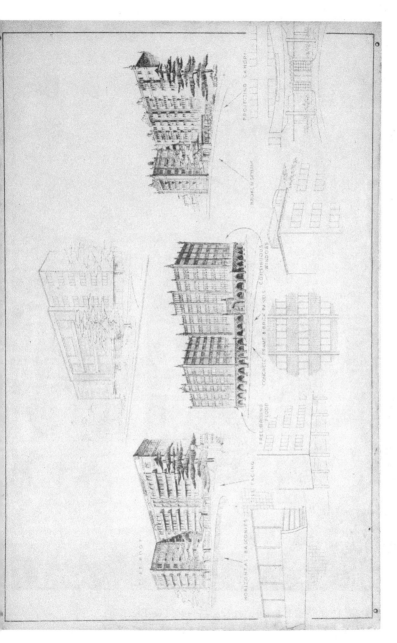

Figure 2.1 Highpoint II, North Hill, Highgate, London: perspectives of proposed block and three others in earlier "styles" but incorporating modern details. Used with permission from RIBApix.

Figure 2.2 Highpoint II façade "effects." Photo: Leo Eigen.

to be impudent. Lubetkin's caryatids were not structural – the canopy is cantilevered and the classical additions serve no functional role. As part of a mostly modern structure and companion to an international style prototype, the caryatids are both far from rational and far from an earnest return to a safe, historical style. Lubetkin's calculated reasoning merely emphasizes how unnecessary he knows his choice to have been. If Lubetkin were truly concerned for the architectural welfare of the 1940s man in the street – there is no evidence he was, but Richards seemed to think this was the case – the retention of a historical or vernacular detail he disingenuously proposed at first would have sufficed. Lubetkin had never directly renounced the importance of architectural history or tradition, but the caryatids are aggressive, their strangeness and absurdity a way for Lubetkin to throw back at the Highgate Preservation Society, the group that had overseen the design process, the rules they had imposed on him. Lubetkin's attention to history here is a history in quotation marks, a sort of Brechtian approach to historical references, and the caryatids are flagrantly inapt.[28] Lubetkin was reveling in the way he had undermined the committee, apparently giving them the acceptable and understandable forms they wanted, but still in the overall service of a modernist high-rise and completely without the earnestness with which his proposed neo-Gothic spires had been received.

At the same time, Lubetkin's act goes well beyond spite, and he was far from self-defeating. One purpose of the caryatids was, no doubt, to confront his more progressive colleagues, not just please the preservationists. In 1937, he bemoaned the problems modern architecture faced in England. Building regulations and a world that did not share the ideals of the movement's founding fathers made for a difficult reception. He wrote, "the greatest necessity is architectural criticism . . . to educate the public, and . . . to clarify the ideas of the architects themselves, and to provide them with that common intellectual basis for which the moment is so sadly lacking." Lubetkin felt isolated. Critics were forced to concentrate solely on function, whose inadequacy as a concept Cox had also lamented.[29] Lubetkin was searching for a manifesto, but for colleagues too, here expressed as a "common intellectual basis." Lack of dialogue had made modernist concepts stale, and Lubetkin, always needing his "thesis" and his "social aims," wanted a community of thinkers with whom to engage. Allan has suggested that Highpoint II pointed to Lubetkin's sense of the limits of international style forms. Perhaps, but the ideas had grown pat for others too, and Lubetkin was conceding that no cultural revolution had come of those times. The caryatids were no more out of place than a heroic-age modernist work would have been. Later, in the forties, he looked back on the preceding decades and wrote:

the golden age of modern architecture is over and done with; its cur-
rent trivialities have become dreary and ineffective, its platitudes
increasingly irrelevant, repetitive and shatteringly boring. All attempts
to establish a unity between aesthetic and conceptual values . . . have
been dissipated and finally frittered away.

Such are the tattered remains of a faith that once appeared as a pow-
erful stimulus to change.[30]

A golden age beyond its prime, a loss of meaning, tattered remains.
Modernism, in effect, was in ruins.

Ruins, of course, perpetuate the glory of the past with their picturesque romanticism, but in England in the late thirties and into the forties,
Summerson, Richards, and other members of the progressive architecture
community also saw ruins as suggestive of the future. Ruins sometimes
imparted emotion and furnished grandeur to dilapidation, but also implied
the potentials of what could be, through a "'posthumous' . . . glamour."[31]
Ruins could lead to a reconceived, modernist future. The international style
might have been limiting, but all was not lost; the waning of the great age
of modern architecture was not a definitive end. Completely devoid of any
sentimentality, Summerson and Richards surveyed the bombed ruins of
England and looked forward to a replanned London. Richards wrote that
the bombings, for instance, are an improvement over "the congested centres
of our cities."[32] This helps us see that Lubetkin was much more allied with
Cox than Cox realized. Highpoint II indeed signaled a change in both the
aesthetic and the social, but the latter had not been prematurely left behind
as Cox had charged. Things were, in fact, moving ahead, even with the
abandonment of sleek modernism. The world around Lubetkin was changing, and his architecture reflected that.

Notes

1　Lubetkin, "Flats in Rosebery Avenue," 140.
2　Among the most accepted of modern architecture's narratives is the clearing
away of its social content upon arriving at MoMA in 1932; Hitchcock and
Johnson directed the focus towards aesthetics, not politics. The English context
was, of course, quite different.
3　Reginald Blomfield, *Modernismus* (London: Macmillan and Co., 1934).
4　George Orwell, "England Your England," in Orwell, *The Lion and the Unicorn:
Socialism and the English Genius* (London: Secker & Warburg, 1941), 9–55.
5　On the assumption in thirties England that British artistic forms and those of
other nationalities were discrete entities, see Keith Holz, *Modern German Art
for Thirties Paris, Prague, and London* (Ann Arbor: University of Michigan
Press, 2004), 136–42. Concerning Abercrombie, see Ken Young and Patricia
L. Garside, *Metropolitan London: Politics and Urban Change 1837–1981*

(London: Edward Arnold Publishers Ltd., 1982), 212. There is a vast body of scholarship on attitudes toward the foreign (both in the arts and in the culture at large) during interwar and wartime Britain. See for instance Pat Kirkham, "Public Opinion During World War II," in Kirkham and David Thoms, eds., *War Culture: Social Change and Changing Experience in World War II* (London: Lawrence & Wishart, 1995). There is also a large body of work addressing English nationalism and the arts; Nikolaus Pevsner's formulation of a particularly English attitude toward art is of course the most well known; his 1955 BBC Reith Lectures were published as *The Englishness of English Art* (Harmondsworth: Penguin, 1956) and will be discussed in the last chapter of this book. Also see: David Getsy, "Locating Modern Art in Britain," *Art Journal* (Winter 2001): 98–102 for an overview of some of the literature in this area; Andrew Causey, ed., *Paul Nash: Writings on Art* (Oxford: Oxford University Press, 2000), especially Nash's discussion of whether it is even possible to be modern and British at the same time; David Peters Corbett and Lara Perry, eds., *English Art 1860–1914: Modern Artists and Identity* (Manchester: Manchester University Press, 2000; New Brunswick: Rutgers University Press, 2001); and Corbett, Ysanne Holt, and Fiona Russell, eds., *The Geographies of Englishness: Landscape and the National Past, 1880–1940* (New Haven and London: Yale University Press, 2002).

6 Keith Aitken, Letter to the editor, *The Architects' Journal* 81 (1935): 159–60; also quoted in Jackson, *Politics of Architecture*, 67.

7 Malcolm Muggeridge, *The Thirties: 1930–40 in Great Britain* (London: Hamish Hamilton, 1940), 240–1.

8 Pierre Vago, *Une vie intense* (Brussels: Editions AAM [Archives d'Architecture Moderne], 2000), 256.

9 On Herbert Read see Jane Beckett, "Circle: The Theory and Patronage of Constructive Art in the Thirties," in Jeremy Lewison, ed., *Circle: Constructive Art in Britain 1934–40* (Cambridge: Kettle's Yard Gallery, 1982), 16; for discussions of the refugees within artistic circles, see John Willett, "The Emigration and the Arts," in Gerhard Hirschfeld, ed., *Exile in Great Britain: Refugees from Hitler's Germany* (Leamington Spa: Berg Publishers/The German Historical Institute and Atlantic Highlands: The Humanities Press, 1984), 105–217; Dennis Sharp, "Framing the Welfare State," *Zodiac* 16 (November 1996): 56–75; for a more general overview, see Daniel Snowman, *The Hitler Émigrés: The Cultural Impact on Britain of Refugees from Nazism* (London: Chatto & Windus, 2002). For political responses to the refugees, see for instance Colin Holmes, "British Government Policy Towards Wartime Refugees," in Martin Conway and Jose Gotovitch, eds., *Europe in Exile: European Exile Communities in Britain 1940–1945* (New York: Berghahn Books, 2001), 11–34. For a discussion of the émigrés in Britain that downplays the gravity of the situation, see Anatole Kopp, "Émigration des architectes, Architecture de l'émigration," in his book *Quand le moderne n'était pas un style mais un cause* (Paris: École nationale supérieure des Beaux-Arts, 1988), 253–314. A symposium in London in 2002 focused on the émigré architecture community, and a recurring question raised by the participants was whether qualities of "foreignness" and "émigré-ness" were identifiable in the work these architects produced. The question was, predictably, declared unanswerable (*Exile and Refuge: The Influence of Refugee and Émigré Architects on British and International Architecture*, organized by the RIBA, at the London Jewish Cultural Centre, June 16, 2002). For some

theorizations surrounding issues of exile and emigration, see Stephanie Barron, ed., *Exiles and Émigrés: The Flight of European Artists from Hitler* (New York: Harry N. Abrams, 1997). This is a vast field of study that will be taken up in the final chapter of this book.

10 Janet Wolff, "The Impolite Boarder: 'Diasporist' Art and its Critical Response," in James Aulich and John Lynch, eds., *Critical Kitaj: A Critical Anthology of Essays on the Work of R.B. Kitaj* (New Brunswick: Rutgers University Press, 2001), 36. Margaret Garlake writes of Jews being told to be "as invisible as possible" to avoid fanning the flames of anti-Semitism, and refers to Tony Kushner's studies that showed that many English people blamed Jews for anti-Semitism for refusing to assimilate, in Garlake, "A Minor Language? Three Émigré Sculptors and their Strategies of Assimilation," in Shulamith Behr and Marian Malet, eds., *Arts in Exile in Britain 1933–1945: Politics and Cultural Identity* (London: University of London/Rodopi, 2004), 173. Louise London challenges the idea that England readily accepted the refugees in London, *Whitehall and the Jews, 1933–1948: British Immigration Policy, Jewish Refugees and the Holocaust* (Cambridge: Cambridge University Press, 2000). On domestic anti-Semitism in Britain and various factions among the Anglo-Jewish community, see Richard Bolchover, *British Jewry and the Holocaust* (Oxford: The Littman Library of Jewish Civilization, 2003). Also see Janet Wolff, "The 'Jewish Mark' in English Painting: Cultural Identity and Modern Art," in Corbett and Perry, *English Art 1860–1914*, 180–94.

11 H.G. Wells's *Anticipations of the Reaction of Mechanical and Scientific Progress Upon Human Life and Thought* (London: Chapman & Hall, 1902) is but one work that shows how ingrained anti-Semitism was in British culture, with casual references to Jews as vulgar, inferior, and curious throughout the book; Orwell's essay is "Anti-Semitism in Britain," *England Your England and Other Essays* (London: Secker & Warburg, 1953), 68–80. Also see J.B.S. Haldane, *Possible Worlds and Other Essays* (London: Chatto & Windus, 1930 [1927]), 154–5 as another example of entrenched, established anti-Semitism among academic, intellectual worlds. Although he was a prominent scientist who actually worked with Lubetkin, Haldane's writings and studies promoted eugenics and this particular text is blatantly anti-Semitic.

12 Romy Golan, "The 'École Française' vs. the 'École de Paris': The Debate about the Status of Jewish Artists in Paris Between the Wars," in Kenneth E. Silver and Romy Golan, eds., *The Circle of Montparnasse: Jewish Artists in Paris 1905–1945* (New York: The Jewish Museum/Universe Books, 1985), 80–7; for Wolff's discussion see "The Impolite Boarder," 1–28.

13 David Elliott, "Gropius in England," in Charlotte Benton, ed., *A Different World: Émigré Architects in Britain 1928–1958* (London: RIBA Heinz Gallery, 1995), 107–23; Senter, "Moholy-Nagy in England"; Christina Thomson, "Contextualizing the Continental: The Work of German Émigré Architects in Britain, 1933–45" (Ph.D. diss., University of Warwick, 1999). For a general overview, see Benton, *A Different World*. Holz downplays the difficulties Gropius, Moholy-Nagy, and Marcel Breuer encountered; Holz, *Modern German Art*, 134.

14 "The New R.I.B.A. Refugee Committee," *Journal of the Royal Institute of British Architects* 46 (February 6, 1939): 324.

15 Charlotte Benton, lecture given at the conference *Exile and Refuge: The Influence of Refugee and Émigré Architects on British and International*

Architecture, organized by the Royal Institute of British Architects at the London Jewish Cultural Centre, June 16, 2002. Also see John Gold, *The Experience of Modernism: Modern Architects and the Future City 1928–1933* (New York and London: E&FN Spon, 1997), 91–2.

16 Susan Harries, *Nikolaus Pevsner: The Life* (London: Chatto & Windus, 2011), 251.

17 The question is a paraphrase of one asked by Benjamin H.D. Buchloh, discussing postwar art in Germany: "How could the condition of an almost complete repression of the memory of having inflicted the holocaust and the devastation of war on a geopolitical and cultural formation previously considered the 'bourgeois humanist civilization' of the European continent *not* affect the definition and the practices of postwar cultural production in that country?" in Buchloh, *Neo-Avantgarde and Culture Industry: Essays on European and American Art from 1955 to 1975* (Cambridge, MA and London: The MIT Press, 2000), xx. The question is also inspired by W.G. Sebald, *On the Natural History of Destruction*, trans. Anthea Bell (London: Penguin, 2003 [1999]), which considers the inadequacy with which postwar Germany's writers addressed their country's World War II atrocities and crimes.

18 RIBA F&D/1/5. Fiona Russell questions the sense that the émigrés influenced modern architecture in England, in "John Ruskin, Herbert Read and the Englishness of British Modernism," in Corbett et al., *Geographies of Englishness*, 303–21. For an opposing view on the importance of émigrés within the modern arts communities of interwar London, see Robin Kinross, "Émigré Graphic Designers in Britain: Around the Second World War and Afterwards," *Journal of Design History* 3 no. 1 (1990): 35–57.

19 Lubetkin, "Modern Architecture in England," 29.

20 Harries, *Nikolaus Pevsner*, 249.

21 *Towards a New Britain:* Exhibition Catalogue for the Royal Institute of British Architects show *The Rebuilding of Britain* (London: The Architectural Press, 1942), 3.

22 Diehl, "Theory and Principle" focuses on ambiguity as a sufficient explanation; Coe and Reading note Lubetkin's "mischief"; Coe and Reading, *Lubetkin and Tecton*, 155.

23 Le Corbusier, "The Vertical Garden City," 10.

24 E.J. Carter and Ernö Goldfinger, *The County of London Plan Explained* (London: Penguin, 1945) refers to Gropius freely. A general theme of Glendinning and Muthesius's *Tower Block* suggests that by the forties in England, once flats were accepted as a housing type, the debate was no longer "flats vs. houses," but instead "how high should the flats go?" to use their terms. In 1952, a BBC program devoted to discussing Lubetkin's Priory Green Estate, London, confirms this. Robert Furneaux-Jordan said on air, "if we're to give space to playgrounds, gardens, let alone the mere admission of light and air, we must build high"; transcript of BBC program, "The Critics," Sunday August 3, 1952, in RIBA LuB/3/3/1. Most of the comments in the broadcast are in favor of building tall in order to provide residents with light and air, and the city with monumental skylines.

25 Allan, *Lubetkin*, 294–5; he acknowledges, though, that the attention to these formal elements is at the expense of a discussion of their "structural origins."

26 Alan Powers, "'The Reconditioned Eye': Architects and Artists in English Modernism," *AA Files* 25 (Summer 1993): 54–62.

27 Mary McLeod has in fact placed Lubetkin within this larger tendency; the phrase "less *sachlich*" is hers, specifically in reference to Lubetkin. See McLeod, "Urbanism and Utopia: Le Corbusier from Regional Syndicalism to Vichy" (Ph.D. diss., Princeton University, 1985), 422. For a negative assessment of this trend, see Banham, for instance, who calls the English architecture of this period the "blunting" of an "intellectual attack" (Banham, *New Brutalism*, 13). A typical example of the tendency to separate British ("radically anti-modern") and non-British humanisms in modern architecture is Sarah Williams Goldhagen, "Coda: Reconceptualizing the Modern," in Goldhagen and Réjean Legault, eds., *Anxious Modernisms: Experimentation in Postwar Architectural Culture* (Cambridge, MA: The MIT Press; Montreal: The Canadian Centre for Architecture, 2000), 317–18.

28 Romy Golan refers to Le Corbusier's self-consciously rusticated thirties work as "materials in quotation marks," in "A 'Discours aux Architectes'?" *Rivista de Arquitectura* 5 (June 2003): 154.

29 Lubetkin, "Modern Architecture in England," 30.

30 RIBA LuB/11/4/1, letter to Monica Felton (Labour Party activist) dated July 17, 1947.

31 E.W., "Two Notes on the Cult of Ruins," Part I, "Ruins and Echoes"; Part II "Utopian Ruins," *Journal of the Warburg Institute* 1 (1937–8): 259–60. Also see Summerson, "Ruins and the Future," *The Listener* 25 (April 17, 1941): 563–4; Summerson, "The Past in the Future," lecture delivered at Bristol University in 1947 and reprinted in Summerson, *Heavenly Mansions and Other Essays on Architecture* (New York: W.W. Norton and Company, 1998), 219–42.

32 Richards, "Foreword to the First Edition," in Richards and Summerson, *The Bombed Buildings of Britain: Second Edition Recording the Architectural Casualties Suffered During the Whole Period of Air Bombardment, 1940–45* (London: The Architectural Press, 1947), 8.

3 High modernist critiques

In the postwar years, Lubetkin concentrated on large housing schemes commissioned by the London County Council (LCC), his work and writings revealing his continued focus on research and his faith in architecture's social potential, even though he retreated more and more from the public pronouncements that characterized his earlier years in London. Highpoint II's loosening up of the international style is indeed an acknowledgment of a moment that had passed, but it ushers in a new phase in which Lubetkin explicitly considers housing in relation to London. While Le Corbusier had seen a potential role for Highpoint I at the level of the city, it was not until the Highpoint II years and after that Lubetkin became involved in planning on a broad scale.

On the cusp of World War II, Lubetkin and Tecton had been commissioned by the London borough of Finsbury to design a comprehensive scheme that addressed housing as well as other needs such as healthcare, education, and community activities – architecture integrated with social reforms.[1] The aforementioned ARP proposals, in fact, were provisions the borough's residents were to be offered as part of the redevelopment scheme. The Finsbury Health Centre (1938) was the only part of the scheme built before war broke out and was extensively written about in the January 1939 issue of *The Architectural Review* as both an aesthetic and social success. Highpoint II, with its provocative exterior, was exactly contemporary to Lubetkin's involvement with town planning, this time moving beyond the paper proposals of the ATO.

During the war, though, the Finsbury area was badly hit by bombings and much of the original Finsbury proposal was scaled back or eliminated. Plans for housing proceeded, with modifications from the prewar intentions; bombs had enlarged some sites, and new zoning laws had altered road layouts and legislated the lowering of population densities. The resulting project, the Spa Green Estate, was completed in 1950 and contains three blocks of flats set into a triangular site with gardens, lawns, and areas for children to play (Figure 3.1).

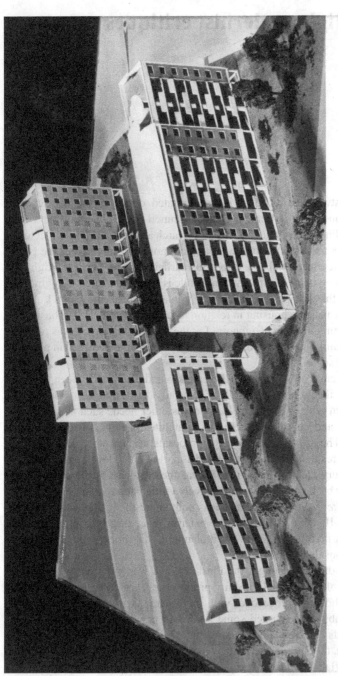

SPA GREEN HOUSING SCHEME, ROSEBERY AVENUE, FINSBURY   TECTON 1944–1948

Figure 3.1 Model of the Spa Green housing scheme, Rosebery Avenue, Finsbury, London: aerial view of the estate. Used with permission from RIBApix.

The existing terraced housing along Rosebery Avenue, one of the main streets that borders the site, meets up with Sadler House, the low-rise block in the estate. Old cedes to new, and Sadler House, with its sinewy footprint, leads the user down into the site along a winding path. The three blocks are set into open space, providing a respite from the surrounding activity. Highpoint II's exterior might have turned some modernist heads, but the tower blocks at Spa Green went further in distancing themselves from thirties forms and embodied what Lubetkin referred to as elevational freedom (Figure 3.2).[2]

A completely animated façade took over each building, leading to formal analyses even more detailed than those that had taken on Highpoint II; Richards, for instance, discussed "surface aesthetics."[3] Writing of the exteriors, Lubetkin resembled a visual artist, his terminology invoking contrasts in light and dark in the manner of a painter discussing chiaroscuro, solids and voids set against each other as a sculptor might think of negative space. He explained the Spa Green façades as follows:

> the overall dynamic pattern is obtained by the introduction of a recessed balcony, the deep slate colour of which underlines the contrast between this plane and the rest of the elevation. The balustrades of these balconies, in contrast, are faced with light-coloured tiles to bring them forward. The solid and void of balustrades alternates from floor to floor, to give an overall rhythm, which allows the elevation to be perceived as a closed composition, rather than as a series of strips.[4]

Pattern, colour, solid, void, rhythm – the language feels painterly and emotive, hardly that of someone whose main concern is to "build socialistically." But at the same time, Lubetkin also offered rational, functional justifications for his decisions, and, as if responding to Richards, wrote that "such attempts at elevational treatment have nothing in common with mere surface pattern-making."[5] Garden façades differed from those looking toward the neighborhood and reflected the quiet space of the bedrooms, while the liveliness of the façades with balconies echoed the bustle of the street. For Lubetkin, his challenge had been "to find a form of expression entirely characteristic of blocks of flats," but certainly in the manner of Le Corbusier's functional yet sculptural *brises-soleils*, an artistic dynamism, called "patternomania" by *Architectural Design*, is part of the point.[6]

The checkerboard patterns, and Lubetkin's detailed explanations for them, dominated his other postwar housing schemes as well, such as Holford Square (1946–54), Priory Green (1943–57), and the Hallfield Estate (1946–54), all in London (Figure 3.3).

Banham acknowledged that "routine-minded modernists" might be "alarmed . . . [or] embarrassed" by Lubetkin's work at Hallfield, as the

Figure 3.2 Spa Green façade. Photo: Leo Eigen.

Figure 3.3 Bevin Court, Holford Square: checkerboard façade detail. Photo: Leo Eigen.

exteriors seem as if they had "been treated as artistic works in their own right" as opposed to being "forced upon the designer by structural, technical or functional considerations."[7] But Banham worked through the buildings and declared them "communicable" and successful, agreeing that Lubetkin's sociological and functional explanations were not deceptions. Lubetkin was always prepared for a debate, ready with discussions or drawings showing that the final pattern had grown out of a rational process and simply had to be as such, as he had done with Highpoint II's caryatids. Architecture's reflection of the world for which it was intended, his own statement about the Penguin Pool, still mattered.

Lubetkin's later papers hint that he might have known he was protesting too much, his annotations revealing that what pleased him about baroque architecture was an apparent disconnect between form and function. He appreciated a "freedom of choice" in the baroque.[8] Aesthetic detailings had always been a priority, from the arabesque balconies on Highpoint I to, indeed, the caryatids of Highpoint II, both of which reappear at least in spirit in his postwar housing estates, with their grand, ceremonial entranceways as well as their patterned façades. The monumental, spiraling, Constructivist-inspired sculptural stairway in the foyer of Bevin Court, one of the tower blocks at the Holford Square Estate, is one such element, beyond mere expressive detail or decorative flourish (Figure 3.4).

The staircase is an organizing principle at the scale of the structure as a whole, the central hinge of the building. Lubetkin called these features "intellectual" in his notes, where he also made comparisons between Pablo Picasso's collages and the balustrades on Francesco Borromini's San Carlo alle Quattro Fontane (1638–41), leading to the conclusion that a viewer must be able to dissociate each element from the whole and notice it individually, but when details are synthesized into "ensembles," the entire experience is new.[9]

Similarly, in an interview in *The Architectural Review* in 1951, Lubetkin drew attention to his buildings as assemblages of parts.[10] He came to describe entire housing schemes in these terms as well; a "homogeneous whole" designed in sections, each building "complete in itself" is how he explained, in 1947, the Bishops Bridge Housing Scheme (the early name for the Hallfield Estate) near Paddington Station.[11] This description brings us right back to the urban theories of Le Corbusier's Radiant City; Lubetkin in fact referred to his residential buildings at Spa Green as "*unités*," emphasizing he was fully aware of the potential significance of his scheme for town planning and postwar reconstruction in London in general, and giving himself quite a prominent lineage in the process.[12] Of course Le Corbusier's Unité d'Habitation in Marseille (1947–52) was meant to be only one element of a larger urban ensemble, and thus we are reminded of

Figure 3.4 Flats in Holford Square, Finsbury, London: view showing the triaxial plan form of the spiral staircase of Bevin Court. Used with permission from RIBApix.

Le Corbusier's hope that the Highpoints could alter all of London's urban development. What became increasingly important for Lubetkin was the relationship among his housing estates, their sites, and the surrounding city; each needed to be analyzed and valorized separately, but the entirety of the scheme depended upon their interaction.

While Le Corbusier had placed an enormous weight on Lubetkin's work in Highgate, for Lubetkin himself, the focus on London progressed differently. There is a transition in his thinking, and it is significant; initially, the vertical garden city of the thirties was to have been a series of towers placed into open green space, decontextualized and appropriate anywhere. It is unsurprising that Tecton, in its early days, had revered Le Corbusier's *Plan Voisin*, which would have wiped away the historic core of Paris (Figure 3.5).[13]

But the increasing postwar focus on each site *as it was*, on orienting tower blocks to address the surrounding area's character, scale, and traffic patterns, and on taking into account the history of each neighborhood points to Lubetkin's architecture taking up a new, changed relationship with London, considering the particulars of each project over and above general, universalist aspirations. Lubetkin's notes for the Hallfield Estate names nearby Gloucester Terrace (designed by William Kingdom and completed in 1852)

Figure 3.5 Le Corbusier, *La Cité Radieuse – Plan Voisin*, 1925. Banque d'Images, ADAGP/Art Resource, NY. © ARS, NY. Used with permission.

as one of the best examples of Victorian town-planning, and "in our opinion requires most reverent treatment."[14] The past, whether modern or Victorian or ruined or extant, was being reconceived for the postwar world. More and more, Lubetkin's notes and proposals refer to the importance of the city as a whole, beyond a singular architectural structure, abandoning the idea of an "isolated estate design" with the site "terminating at its gates." Instead, Lubetkin and his colleagues wrote that "the organic interpenetration of the estate and its surrounds enriches both,"[15] adjusting the orientation of buildings based largely on the best views both out of, and into, the site. His increasingly animated elevations were rooted in Highpoint II's ornamentations and its aforementioned "visual effects." There is a picturesque air to a concern with vistas, though Lubetkin's apologist Robert Furneaux-Jordan insisted that Lubetkin designed "spatially" not scenographically.[16] Furneaux-Jordan's claims seem valid when we remember that the façade's effects were a link to urban space, the patterned elevations hinting at public versus private spaces, acknowledging the interior function as well as their surroundings. An awareness of the existing urban environment – at Spa Green, for example, the shape of the site echoed the local street layout – enabled Lubetkin to see his housing as perpetuating what he called urban "vitality . . . integrating man and his environment."[17]

It is Lubetkin himself who gives us the right to base our understanding of his postwar tower blocks on Highpoint II. To him, his projects were simply continuations of investigations already in progress, initiated by preceding work. A short piece he wrote for *The Architectural Review* in 1951 begins with an unsigned introduction that claims the flats at Spa Green "represent but one stage in a process of working out a certain philosophy of exterior design which can only properly be understood in relation to previous and subsequent designs by the same architects," followed by his claim that the innovations of Spa Green evolved in relation to those in Highpoint II.[18] By looking at his work as a series, we can see that although the caryatids indeed appear detached from Lubetkin's earlier political theses, they legitimize the looser vocabulary of his later work, confirming Highpoint II as a pivotal moment and offering a connection to the postwar work and its attention to the city. Highpoint II, then, also links his postwar housing to Le Corbusier's original reading of Highpoint I: Lubetkin's concerns were urban and wide-reaching. This is hardly a world on hiatus.

The postwar estates' patterned elevations, Lubetkin's justifications of the process by which they came about, and his focus on architectural work as socially-minded and an ensemble made up of an assemblage of parts can also all be traced back to his Russian Constructivist days, when the use of materials in three-dimensional art objects as well as three-dimensionality itself as an artistic phenomenon had both intrigued him. Again, the focus on *tektonika* is more spatial than purely visual; on several occasions in Moscow, Lubetkin had lectured on *faktura* in Vladimir Tatlin's art; that is, the choice of material and the working of it "as a whole."[19] Lubetkin's Constructivist heritage once again made its way into his work; as captured in Tatlin's iconic *Corner Counter-Relief* (1914–15) sculpture, Constructivist art rejected the idea of art as an autonomous, hermetic object, instead extending itself outward to incorporate and interact with real three-dimensional space. This was the way the Constructivist revolutionaries announced they would rebuild and redesign the world. Lubetkin, too, gave architecture an expansive definition, far from the pure formalism a checkerboard façade might imply. Lubetkin's postwar estates might have been about surface aesthetics to Richards, but they fulfilled modernist social ambitions remarkably fully. Cox was wrong to have criticized Lubetkin for a moral breach; it was simply untenable to perpetuate outdated forms. Lubetkin's forties and fifties work was still modern in its totality, its attention to social obligations such as large-scale housing, and its search for new aesthetics and concerns, all of which appeared throughout these projects.

The Busaco Street housing scheme, for example, whose planning began just before the war and was later called Priory Green, was one such innovative new form. It contained flats in six-story blocks with elevator access to the upper floors. Partially influenced by economics – elevators were not a given at this time and the LCC had to approve the added expense – Tecton proposed that the lift would only stop on the ground and third floors, with access to other floors by way of stairs. The third floor would be a mid-block central gathering place for tenants, allowing for face-to-face contact among residents and adding a social purpose to the limited use of elevators. Notes for the project indicate that the proposed height, the use of lifts, and the third-floor quasi-public corridor were all unusual additions that set the architects up for rejection from the LCC. The Council in fact approved the project, but it was tabled during the war and subsequently scaled down, making the lifts and thus the third-floor expanded corridor unnecessary.

In 1952, Lubetkin, having by this time disbanded Tecton and formed the practice Skinner, Bailey, and Lubetkin, submitted an entry to the Golden Lane housing competition. Golden Lane has become significant in modern architectural lore not because of the winning design, an almost forgotten mixed development scheme by Chamberlain, Powell, and Bon, nor because of Lubetkin's firm's proposal, but because of Alison and Peter Smithson's now-iconic submission (Figure 3.6).

Marilyn Monroe and Joe DiMaggio cavorting on a "street-deck" secured the Smithsons' important place in the narrative of the postwar architectural avant-garde. Recognizable figures from popular culture implied inclusivity and a denunciation of the illegible, elite abstraction of high modernism.

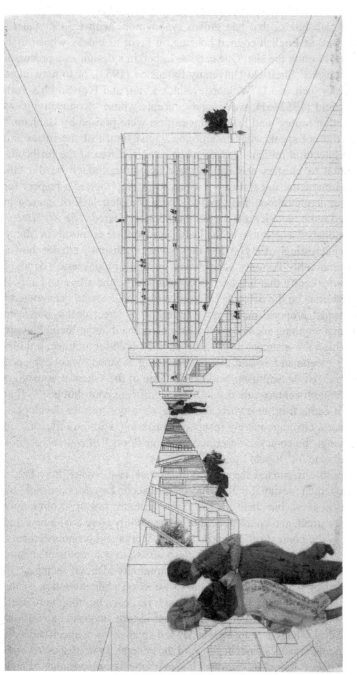

Figure 3.6 Alison and Peter Smithson, Golden Lane, London Deck, Perspective Photomontage, 1952. Photo: Jean-Claude Planchet/ G. Meguerditchian. Location: Musee National d'Art Moderne, Centre Georges Pompidou, Paris. © CNAC/MNAM/Dist. RMN-Grand Palais/Art Resource, NY. Used with permission.

Yet those ideas are also contained within Lubetkin's scheme, which rejected the linear slab blocks that had grown synonymous with Le Corbusier's *unités* as well as English council housing, in favor of blocks whose footprints wind through the site. One can see Lubetkin's design as a precursor to the Smithsons' Sheffield University Extension (1953), or to networked tower blocks such as J.L. Womersley, Jack Lynn, and Ivor Smith's Park Hill, Sheffield (1953–61), works and concepts whose "'connectivity' of the circulation routes" and lack of linear form were praised by Banham.[20] Lubetkin did not speak what became the lingua franca of the fifties and sixties architectural milieu – his language remained free of the forthcoming attention to clusters and habitats and networks, though he did talk about environmental integration – but his form grew out of a respect for the existing neighborhood and city life, and a complete lack of interest in the isolated *unité*, convictions the Smithsons later shared. *The Architects' Journal* published a selection of the losing competition proposals in March 1952, and interestingly, the pop drawings by the Smithsons were not shown, but their remarkably Tectonesque elevation on a linear block was, a detail of the Smithsons' entry that has been overshadowed by the allure and appeal of the celebrities on the balcony.[21] Significantly, the *Journal*'s coverage of the Smithsons' proposal makes no mention of its street decks, nor even suggests that anything seemed particularly significant about them, belying the fascination those streets-in-the-air eventually held for architectural history. Peter Eisenman has said that the "building as street" was developed by Peter and Alison Smithson, and calls it "one of the salient propositions of mid-twentieth-century urbanism . . . [a] significant contribution."[22] That it is, but it came from elsewhere, and they were not its sole developers. The *Journal*'s coverage merely mentions in passing, with no reflection on their meaning, "balconies . . . each serving three floors," of course Tecton's original scheme for Busaco Street.[23]

The Smithsons entered the picture in the late 1940s when they began working on their design for the Hunstanton Secondary Modern School, completed in 1954, but their allegedly new attitudes towards community life, the city street, and an awareness of urban vitality were not so new and fit firmly in the context of Lubetkin's earlier works and pronouncements. Even Peter Smithson's conception of "*the building as a* component and not as a monument. Of building towards the community idea. Of facing up to the new sort of scale"[24] is comparable to Lubetkin's identification of the several levels on which architecture operated; i.e., each building unto itself mattered, but contributed to an ensemble that in turn suggested a relationship to the city. The shared move was toward an analysis of specific needs, away from modernism's tendency toward the general, as we discussed with his LCC estates.[25] Lubetkin's postwar housing schemes are critiques of high modernism in ways that are aligned with the Smithsons' growing frustration with, and yet obsession with, an older generation of CIAM architects. Lubetkin's language and focus, highlighting the "un-monumental English working class streets,"[26] were coopted by them in their drive to undo the urbanism in which they had been steeped as young students.

In 1953, in Aix-en-Provence, the ninth meeting of CIAM was held, Alison and Peter Smithson the main representatives of the MARS Group. The Smithsons presented their Golden Lane proposal, rallied for an urbanism based on "human associations" rather than the strict functional zoning Le Corbusier had sought to promulgate, spoke of the "vital sense of communal life," and, as succinctly summarized by Joan Ockman, highlighted the city as a place of the "nitty-gritty of 'reality' . . . to counteract the diagrammatic and static purism of Athens Charter urbanism," referring to the 1933 document that had codified Le Corbusier's form of Cartesian city planning.[27] The ideas were published the following year as the Doorn Manifesto, the publication and its subsequent unleashing of the ire, arrogance, and activity of the younger generation responsible for the final dissolution of CIAM and its reformulation into the Smithsons-led Team Ten. Yet, every single one of these ideas, credited for completely changing the course of postwar European architectural theory, was considered by, articulated by, and presented by Lubetkin.

Lubetkin embarked on these critiques in 1938, with Highpoint II. The difference, of course, is that Lubetkin was of that earlier era, whereas the Smithsons were the youngsters, bursting onto the scene and apparently criticizing what had come before. But Lubetkin lacked the collaborative strength or support of a think tank such as the MARS Group, which he had rejected. MARS, of course, provided the entrée to the international scene for the Smithsons. The move from Lubetkin's generation and its ideas to the fifties and the Smithsons was fluid and gradual, not a clear-cut rupture.

The Smithsons were master provocateurs even apart from the backing they received from Banham, their great champion for a time, whereas by 1939, Lubetkin had moved to a farm in Gloucestershire. He maintained his London practice, but he opted out of the vocal, confrontational style of his prewar years, and an avant-garde needs bluster. Lubetkin's daughter clearly connects this to an absolute need to deny the fate befalling his parents and millions of Jews left in Europe, to tune it all out with deep, deep self-deception. Banham's whole conception of the New Brutalism, which he distilled into a casual "*je-m'en-foutisme*" (his own rough translation is "bloody-mindedness")[28] and the sense that Brutalist architecture was nearly "a brick-bat flung in the public's face,"[29] perfectly captured the self-consciously, youthfully, angry, rebellious Smithsons. Somehow it is ironic that Alison and Peter Smithson would later group their writings into a book called *Without Rhetoric*[30] when for a time it was simply rhetoric that separated them from Lubetkin, and somehow it is further ironic, if not just bluntly wrong, that his seclusion might be summed up as a quiet pause, when in fact it contained within it the full, active, catastrophic knowledge that his family had been sent to the death camps. In other words, it was anything *but* quiet.

The unquestioned acceptance of the Smithsons as the protagonists and pioneers of the postwar architectural avant-garde needs to be reconsidered as much as Lubetkin's Highpoint II "deviation," to quote Cox, does. Lubetkin was, frankly, of a preceding and different cultural moment. His caryatids are perhaps a form of "brick-bat," and he had a defiant nature similar to that of the Smithsons, but the pop imagery and references to mass culture that they used and adapted and that were going to become unavoidable in the culture at large were simply unavailable to him. On the other hand, he was not completely out of touch. Spa Green's tower blocks were wired for television, and one of the estate's most heavily touted amenities was the Garchey refuse disposal system, invented in France. The system had been used at the Quarry Hill flats in Leeds (1938), designed by R.A.H. Livett, but Spa Green marked its first application in London. The system received much coverage in the architectural press, hailing it for technical and hygienic reasons, and tenants received a special handbook explaining in detail how to dispose of their rubbish.[31]

Lubetkin, it seems, had anticipated the throwaway culture of pop.

Notes

1   Allan, *Lubetkin*, chapter 8.
2   Lubetkin, "Flats in Rosebery Avenue," 140.
3   J.M. Richards, "The Next Step?" *The Architectural Review* 107 (March 1950): 165–81.
4   Lubetkin, "Flats in Rosebery Avenue," 140.
5   Lubetkin, "Flats in Rosebery Avenue," 140. Julius Posener, too, described Spa Green's expression of its structure "instead of *suppressing* it in the name of art," in Posener, "Knots in the Master's Carpet," *Architectural Design* 51 (December 1951): 356. Emphasis original. Posener and others have connected the patterns to textile work from the Caucuses, and Allan traces the grand entranceways at Spa Green to the Russian churches Lubetkin would have seen as a child. Allan, *Lubetkin*, 400.
6   On the form of expression appropriate to flats, see RIBA LuB/1/24 and the notes for the planning of Spa Green; on the increasing importance of expressiveness in modern architecture and housing, see Frederick Gibberd, "Expression in Modern Architecture," *Journal of the Royal Institute of British Architects* 59 (January 1952): 79. Posener credited Le Corbusier for "the present patternomania," in Posener, "Knots in the Master's Carpet," 356.

7 Reyner Banham, "Façade: Elevational Treatment of the Hallfield Estate Paddington," *The Architectural Review* 116 (November 1954): 303–7.

8 RIBA LuB/17/3; the notes are dated 1987.

9 Lubetkin, "Flats in Holford Square, Finsbury," *The Architectural Review* 111 (June 1952): 403–6.

10 Lionel Brett and Berthold Lubetkin, "Canons of Criticism: 2," transcript of a conversation, *The Architectural Review* 109 (March 1951): 136.

11 RIBA LuB/4/9/1, report dated September 16, 1947.

12 Lubetkin, "Flats in Rosebery Avenue."

13 RIBA SaG/90/1, a series of letters exchanged in 1936 among Le Corbusier, RIBA Librarian and ATO member E.J. Carter, and Tecton architect Godfrey Samuel.

14 RIBA LuB/4/9.

15 RIBA LuB/4/9/1, report dated September 16, 1947.

16 Robert Furneaux-Jordan, "Lubetkin," *The Architectural Review* 118 (July 1955): 44.

17 Lubetkin, "Flats in Holford Square."

18 Unsigned introduction to Lubetkin, "Flats in Rosebery Avenue," 138–40.

19 Lodder, *Russian Constructivism*, 99. Lodder also writes that while the literal meaning of the Russian term is "texture," that translation "is inadequate to convey the ideological and artistic overtones which it carries in Russian" (280n.64). The three "tenets" of Russian constructivism require *tektonika* and *faktura* to work in conjunction with *konstruktsiya* (the actual process of construction and structuring). Of course having named the firm Tecton again emphasizes that Lubetkin's interests were not merely aesthetic.

20 Banham, "The New Brutalism," 361.

21 "Golden Lane Competition: A Selection of Unsuccessful Entries," *The Architects' Journal* 115 (March 20, 1952): 358–60. That the Smithsons' Golden Lane proposal looks to Lubetkin's Spa Green is made explicit in Glendinning and Muthesius, *Tower Block*, 121.

22 Peter Eisenman, "From Golden Lane to Robin Hood Gardens: Or If You Follow the Yellow Brick Road, It May Not Lead to Golders Green" (1973) reprinted in Eisenman, *Eisenman Inside Out: Selected Writings 1963–1988* (New Haven: Yale University Press, 2004), 41. Eisenman roots the street decks in Le Corbusier's work, but he absolutely declares they were mainly the brainchild of the Smithsons.

23 "Street decks" were not unusual; they were a common topic among AA students in the early fifties, according to Glendinning and Muthesius, *Tower Block*, 127. Banham explicitly writes that the Smithsons put the idea "back" into circulation ("The New Brutalism," 361).

24 Peter Smithson, "The Idea of Architecture in the '50s," *The Architects' Journal* (January 21, 1960): 122. Emphasis original.

25 Volker Welter questions whether the Smithsons ever really renounced modernist universals in spite of their language otherwise; Welter, "Talking Squares – Grids and Grilles as Architectural, Analytical, and Communicative Tools," in D'Laine Camp, Dirk van den Heuvel, and Gijs de Waal, eds., *Team 10: Between Modernity and the Everyday*, proceedings of a conference organized by the Faculty of Architecture TU Delft, June 2003. The most recent work on the Smithsons is M. Christine Boyer, *Not Quite Architecture: Writing Around Alison and Peter Smithson* (Cambridge, MA: The MIT Press, 2017).

26 Glendinning and Muthesius, *Tower Block*, 127.
27 Joan Ockman and Edward Eigen, eds., *Architecture Culture 1943–1968: A Documentary Anthology* (New York: Columbia University and Rizzoli International Publications, 1993), 181.
28 Banham, "The New Brutalism," 357.
29 Banham, "The New Brutalism," 356.
30 Alison and Peter Smithson, *Without Rhetoric: An Architectural Aesthetic, 1955–1972* (London: Latimer, 1973).
31 *Spa Green Estate: Handbook for Tenants* (London: Finsbury Borough Council, 1949).

4 Practicing Jews

Modern London, the emigration decade, and the weight of history

Vitruvius invoked the Erechtheum's caryatids to justify the obligation of an architect to be knowledgeable of the past, writing that

> wide knowledge of history is requisite because, among the ornamental parts of an architect's design for a work, there are many the underlying idea of whose employment he should be able to explain to inquirers.

The people of Caryae in Peloponnesus had sided with the enemies of Greece, Vitruvius recounted, and as punishment for betraying the state, the Greeks took the married women of Caryae into slavery. Their capture doomed them to a lifetime of indignity, forever binding them to their dishonor. When architects of the day designed statues of the fallen women and placed them on their buildings, it was "in order that the sin and punishment of the people of Caryae might be known and handed down even to posterity." Classical caryatids carried weight – not just structural but historical weight, the literal mass of the building their enduring responsibility as much as the burdens of their past sins and a story about justice and vengeance. Contradicting the glibness that has been attributed to Lubetkin, Highpoint II marked a decisive moment for him, his architecture from that point forward legitimizing a new expressiveness and an interest in urbanism, the transition from a prewar to wartime mindset encapsulated in those caryatids (Figure 4.1).

1938 – the year the first tenants moved into Highpoint II. The year that Austria was annexed by Nazi Germany, the Evian Conference declared that the United States and United Kingdom were closed to Jewish refugees, the Munich Agreement was signed, and Kristallnacht was unleashed. How could Lubetkin's Jewishness not matter? Goldfinger knew the climate he was up against. As his biographer reveals, Goldfinger and his wife had non-Jewish-sounding first names ready for their children just before their births and had even toyed with the idea of changing their surname Goldfinger.[1]

Figure 4.1 Highpoint II, Lubetkin, and the Highpoint II *porte-cochère*. Used with
permission from RIBApix.

We have already discussed that during the thirties and forties it was fashion-
able and respectable to be anti-Semitic and anti-refugee; many Jews hoped to
be as invisible as possible, avoiding what was felt to be the otherwise certain
aggression directed towards them. Remaining inconspicuous and invisible
mattered. Similarly, Highpoint II's caryatids discreetly concealed Lubetkin's
revolutionary, modernist side, couching it in conservative, backwards-
looking, mollifying, historical detailing. Just as the drapery of classical sculp-
tures conceals but reveals the forms of the bodies underneath along with the
mastery of classical artists, Lubetkin's caryatids were, on the surface, quiet
as well, a non-radical form masking the urgency that lurked beneath – the
urgency of a Europe on fire – and focusing instead on comfortable, luxury
housing. 1939 – Lubetkin made his move to the countryside, leaving behind

Highpoint II, a remnant of a revolutionary cry, a ruin of modernism's anti-historical purity. 1940 – Lubetkin's parents, killed in Auschwitz. To slightly tweak the question W.G. Sebald asks postwar Germany: how could this horrifying chapter of history perpetrated upon Lubetkin's family not enter his consciousness? How could it not matter?

It mattered, his daughter has declared, writing about her father's trips to London and his return to Gloucestershire with challah in tow.

> I remembered how he sometimes brought back from London beautiful, shiny loaves of braided bread, whose taste and texture were so different from the bland white pablum which passed for bread in England in those days. "It's Polish bread," he said; and why would I doubt his word? I couldn't have known that it was challah, nor that in buying and eating it he was taking a furtive and lonely trip back to his buried past.[2]

Lubetkin's daughter recounts in her memoirs her discovery of a photograph of the postwar wreckage of her grandparents' home in Warsaw, on Jerusalem Avenue, and the caryatids, amidst the ruins, that dominate the image.[3] Lubetkin had steered anyone who tried to excavate his past in the wrong direction, deliberately misleading researchers into thinking the caryatids that remained in his memory were part of his lodgings as a student at the Warsaw Polytechnic, while in fact they were a much more personal presence than that. Kehoe consulted old phonebooks and determined with confidence that her grandparents' home was the source of the caryatids that had ingrained themselves in his consciousness and made their way to Highgate.[4] "You went back there after the war to try to find your parents, didn't you, Dad, and all you found was the ruined house."[5] Lubetkin's *porte-cochère* covered over his avant-garde fervor and his secret catastrophe, and was part of his strategy to keep quiet and bury the past. Lubetkin, with his classical columns, was offering the Highgate neighborhood an artifact from the British Museum and a remnant of the vast cultural legacy it housed, the strength of old England in a modern tower block of flats. And yet in his own private way, he was declaring his past and his origins. The caryatids were a cover, but far from silent. The drive for modernism in England, the avant-garde community's exhaustive struggle for the new architecture to take root, and the continual debate were anything but quiet. These were serious efforts to change the face of London.

* * *

Modern British architecture has largely been thought of in terms of dichotomies. Mendelsohn's quiet hiatus has led us instead to a time of political turmoil and architectural activity. In the late twenties, Hitchcock had discerned that English architects were aware of the aesthetics of continental modern architecture but did not absorb the ideas behind the new architecture, merely whitewashing the brick and stucco exteriors of their structures.[6] We have documented the thirties in terms of a struggle for modernism; even in the forties and into the fifties, while England became a car-centered, modernized country, architects and designers counterintuitively celebrated the way new, modern highways would result in the preservation "of Old England by making road-widening in picturesque towns and villages unnecessary."[7] Perhaps that dichotomy is most acutely summed up by Erwin Panofsky, like Pevsner a German Jewish émigré in England who analyzed English culture and described Englishness in terms of a now-famous duality between the complex engineering of a Rolls-Royce and the lyricism of the Palladian temple front of its radiator. Panofsky's construct is often quoted, but still resonates.[8] Richards's abandonment of international style modernism, seen in his defense of Highpoint II, was part of this dichotomy, and also parallels the transition in thinking that Pevsner notoriously underwent, what Banham called his mentor's betrayal, laid out in Banham's biting critique of Pevsner's volte-face and *The Architectural Review*'s increasing support for picturesque planning.

Indeed, the international style in England was short-lived and yielded to what Pevsner's biographer called "a softer, more human" sort of architecture.[9] That so-called soft architecture, that dichotomy between revolutionary forms and vernacular forms, nonetheless hid an urgency. The "soft" architecture of the New Empiricism was in fact deeply political in its explicit rejection of the international style and, instead, its embrace of nationalism. Similarly, the exhortation to Jews to quiet down, to remain invisible, was just as political. Lubetkin might have chosen to remain invisible in terms of his Jewishness, but that veil was also forced upon him and other Jews. Out of an oppressive moment, came art, perhaps the most commanding of all the dichotomies discerned here. Art historian Donald Kuspit calls this a "creative Jewishness," a way Jews have inwardly adapted to a society that opposes them, the best art being a result of this "searching conscience."[10]

Pevsner more than anyone created and codified the architectural history of his adopted homeland through his forty-six-volume *Buildings of England* series, searching for a way to characterize Englishness. Pevsner saw the wildness of the English garden as an extension of the English ideals of liberty and freedom, but the staid control and conservativeness of English art as rooted in the country's lack of a revolutionary past. Perhaps Pevsner's obsession with nationalism was an obsession with not being Jewish, a desperate rejection of his outsider status. His biographer claims that converting from Judaism was a way for him to ignore the solidarity of a community.

One could also say it was, therefore, a way to embrace such a solidarity – to become English, to become part of England as a community, and to fit into English culture and to make sense of this new place.

Lubetkin was not just part of the modernist scene in London – he helped create and promote it, along with the many Jews with whom he worked in his practice, such as his collaborators Peter Moro, Godfrey Samuel, Carl Ludwig Franck, and Denys Lasdun, shaping the landscape of mid-century London, their work and theories directing much of the influential output of the postwar avant-garde. Moro and Franck, for instance, were refugees from Nazi Germany; both were interned as enemy aliens before working with Lubetkin. Franck was a master draftsman responsible for many of Tecton's detailed presentation drawings. Moro, whose design for the Royal Festival Hall was influenced by Tecton's Finsbury Health Centre, was taken in by Lubetkin when Gropius allegedly reneged on a promise to his fellow countryman.[11] Long before Lasdun's Royal National Theatre (1976) changed the South Bank of the Thames, his 1951 Hallfield Primary School (an offshoot of Tecton's Hallfield Estate undertaking) experimented with strong concrete forms expressing the building's structure, ideas that were simultaneously taken up by the Smithsons at Hunstanton. Lasdun, in fact, changed the language of postwar architecture as early as 1954, adopting what historians called a "crushing rhetoric" to describe a new social theory inherent in his Bethnal Green "cluster blocks." A non-rectangular tower block with corridors meeting at a central core, these blocks gave way to new urban concepts – the term "vertical street," the "urban grain" of the city, the idea that urban planning should be based in the "natural aggregation" of people and communities.[12]

Fredric Bedoire has considered the impact of Jews on modern European architecture, though his study ends in 1930 and is only marginally concerned with England.[13] To paraphrase him, though: London would have looked very different without the Jews. It goes well beyond mere patronage; Gestetner, from whom the Highpoints emerged, was Jewish, and relatedly, a recent study of the French Jewish architect Pierre Chareau evaluated his Jewishness mainly in terms of his patrons, in spite of the fact that around him, German forces were invading the streets of Paris.[14] It is simply not enough to stop there. Nor is it enough that the architects were Jewish; this is not intended merely as a list of architects of Jewish heritage who worked in London, nor could one ever seek to say the architecture "looked Jewish," whatever that could possibly mean. Rather, the architecture created during these anything-but-paused years was part of a time of urgency and great activity. And much of that urgency and activity can be connected to a Jewish presence in London. The cultural moment produced internments, suspicions, fears, anxieties, partnerships, and indeed, architecture.

Out of oppression came art. Lara Trubowitz has argued that anti-Semitism defined the artistic world of modern Britain – Virginia Woolf's work is inseparable, for instance, from her degrading descriptions of Jewish characters – and Lubetkin worked within that world.[15] Similar to the question Trubowitz poses for literature, did an architectural response to underlying anti-Semitism and the outsider status of Jews and foreigners help push and promote a modernist agenda in architecture?

In 1964, Sibyl Moholy-Nagy, wife of refugee artist László Moholy-Nagy, referred to the thirties in England as the "emigration decade" during a conference on modern architecture at Columbia University.[16] The term is appropriate to describe the diaspora of refugee intellectuals that formed the context to Lubetkin's career, though Moholy-Nagy also dissected what she saw as a loss of critical edge in the work of some of the refugees (singling out Mendelsohn and Pevsner for her discussion) when they were transplanted to their new English homeland. The sense that émigré intellectuals and artists become deradicalized during migration is debated extensively in the scholarship of emigration studies, and the field of diaspora studies as well takes up various interpretations of the relationship between the cultures of the host country and the refugee's original homeland, more often than not seen as vague and fluid and elusive. Even an attempt to put down roots becomes, in many formulations of exile theory, an "essential sadness."[17] This is the conflict Pevsner articulated for himself, one between separation and belonging, between migration and taking root.

Besides Sibyl Moholy-Nagy, other scholars have also referred in passing to the significance of the thirties European refugees to the history of modern architecture. In their two-volume work *Modern Architecture*, Manfredo Tafuri and Francesco Dal Co write that a

> nonmarginal role in the diffusion of the modern architectural language was played by the architects who, after the advent of Nazism, left Germany to settle in England or the United States. This diaspora, along with the hagiographic interpretation of the great days of CIAM, has encouraged the myth of the "progressive" vocation of the modern movement.[18]

Loss of a critical edge, essential sadness, the *dépaysé* artist, hagiography, myth – these are suggestive notions, with an aura of gravitas that in some ways remains in the rarefied realm of the poetic and only loosely addresses the very real cultural anxiety and urgency that pervaded British society during the time Lubetkin became an émigré. That the RIBA Refugee Committee saw the exiles as "problems" is far removed from an abstract, lyrical formulation of deracination.

What does Jewish émigré architecture look like? Certainly England provided relative freedom for artistic undertakings, no small contribution, and in 1937, Sigfried Giedion expressed his belief that England and the United States were the most viable artistic havens now that Europe was crumbling.[19] Carol Zemel's recent book *Looking Jewish* seeks to study the experience of diasporist Jews as captured in art; Lubetkin and others are part of that experience, the diaspora of modern architecture as contained in the dissemination of ideals that originated on continental Europe, traveled to England, and encountered a storm of anti-Semitism in spite of the liberties offered.[20] How can we attempt to theorize the "emigration decade" and the interaction among England, Jewishness, and this diaspora of architects?

Perhaps it is no coincidence that émigré architects in thirties London who were conscious of their Jewishness helped define and shape modern London as a place. Lubetkin, we have read, discussed his postwar housing in terms of the city, the housing site responding to the urban environment. Pevsner and Panofsky, of course, delineated and outlined Englishness, seeking a definition of what made England recognizable as England. This quest was also undertaken by Goldfinger, whose path crossed with Lubetkin's often throughout their lives and careers, starting from their early days in Paris working with August Perret and long before the Goldfingers took up residence at Highpoint I. Goldfinger's important concrete towers dominated the skylines of Poplar in east London (Balfron Tower, 1965–7) and Kensal Town in west London (Trellick Tower, 1972) for many years, and he indeed was the stimulus for Ian Fleming when the latter wrote *Goldfinger* and was searching to name James Bond's nemesis. The resulting villainous character, Auric Goldfinger, is described as an émigré from Eastern Europe, and the book is full of anti-Semitic and anti-foreign descriptions and scorn.[21] Fleming hated concrete architecture, and it seems he was no fan of Jews either.

Before working on his towers, Goldfinger helped spread, like Pevsner, a "soft" modernist message when he co-authored with E.J. Carter, the RIBA librarian and MARS member, the *County of London Plan Explained* in 1945. The book was commissioned by the aforementioned planner Patrick Abercrombie to help promote his plan for the reconstruction of London, the *County of London Plan*, a government-sponsored report written in 1943 with J.H. Forshaw. The looseness of Abercrombie's language allowed Carter and Goldfinger to direct the message they wanted to send, and they emphasized what seemed to be a rather slight point: that the average Londoner's participation and action are what would create a renewed city. They urged residents to "think hard about the way they want their lives to be lived; work out the social, economic, physical and political reasons why what they want does not exist in fact; study the Plan intelligently, using their heads as well as their hearts, so that a better London can be achieved."[22] Carter and Goldfinger asserted that the Plan would define new urban "patterns" and "associations" based on the choices of Londoners and their existing communities. Again, these are the terms that Team Ten later used to define their urban theories. First published in 1968, the *Team Ten Primer* talks of all these elements – free choice, city patterns – and quotes its own 1954 Doorn Manifesto: the goal of the architect and planner is "to comprehend the pattern of human associations."[23] The move toward user-based, participatory design articulated by Carter and Goldfinger hinted at a fifties architectural world that was still to come.[24]

The County of London Plan Explained was inflected by a series of essays that Goldfinger had published in *The Architectural Review* in 1941–2. The three essays, "The Sensation of Space," "Urbanism and Social Order," and "Elements of Enclosed Space,"[25] are ultimately concerned with articulating and explaining what Goldfinger calls "spatial emotion," the subconscious psychological effect that architecture has on a person. Goldfinger's definition of architectural space is broad and inclusive, seeing it in social terms that include not just buildings, but city streets and urban spaces as well. In the essays, he emphasized the importance of technology and art, always foregrounding a person's relationship to his community, which he called the "being within," and formed a theory proposing emotive, expressive architecture.[26]

It is relevant to note the focus on "being within," since the sense of being an outsider defined Goldfinger during the time he wrote the essays. His application for British citizenship was delayed and "as a Jew with communist connections," his comfortable position in London society was tenuous, even though his wife was English.[27] Perhaps his essays on defining London through the activity of its citizens and on the human, emotional response to architecture were ways to feel rooted in an upended world of war, where being a refugee or a foreigner or a Jewish person was an inextricable, complicated part of daily life that needed to be navigated.

And perhaps Lubetkin's caryatids and his memory of them were also a way to put down roots, to mitigate his foreignness by way of the British Museum, but in the process angering everyone – modernists and preservationists alike. Ultimately, it was hard for him to remain quiet. Highpoint II parallels Jewish culture during this time, the classical calm of the columns masking what seethed beneath the surface. The refugees were accepted, but with certain qualifications. The caryatids seemed historical and regressive, but what was lurking underneath them was a grappling with international style modernism, with rigorous design concerns, and with newfound attention to more expansive planning issues.

* * *

For architect and theorist Stanley Tigerman, Jewishness is open-ended, looking forward to the coming of the Messiah, always gazing forward and outward. Invoking Jacques Derrida, Tigerman further discusses exile, and Jewish exile in particular, as a completely non-nostalgic, non-romantic way of being, different from the essential sadness mentioned earlier.[28] Lubetkin's architecture, too, was always looking ahead, processing new ideas and developing new forms with little sentimentality. It is not that émigré architecture "looks like" something specific, or has identifiable characteristics, but rather, that the cultural moment that produced these defining works was a cultural moment defined by urgency. Refugees were seeking safety, foreigners were at a loss to defend themselves against certain prejudices or fears, and a society was struggling to make it through wartime. Such a moment was anything but quiet. Bombs altered the cityscape, and architects responded.

If one considers the literature on English modern architecture, there are four main narratives that define the field: first, that the modern architectural climate tended toward a picturesque, anti-urban sentiment; second, that the overriding concern for the common man frustrated experimentation and abstraction; third, that the MARS Group dominated the avant-garde happenings and theorizations; and fourth, that the émigrés were welcomed by the progressive English architectural community though they never quite left a significant impact in the wake of their careers. All of these narratives come together and intertwine to support the overriding claim with which this study began: that modern architecture in England never really took hold.

Yet, each of those narratives is undone by Berthold Lubetkin. Highpoint II is a pivotal moment at which Lubetkin broke from international style modernism and allowed a new focus to take over. This has been a story of Lubetkin, his shaping of London, and his influence on a postwar generation of architectural thinkers. This was a time of architectural experimentation, and also a time of turbulence; in 1938, Highpoint II was complete and Europe was yielding to disaster. The dilemma of being an outsider is summed up in Psalm 137: "How can we sing . . . on foreign soil?" Lubetkin, too, was perpetually asking questions, trying to shape foreign soil and making that sense of open-endedness apt, but as Lubetkin looked ahead, he felt the weight of a hidden past. Indeed, modern London would have looked completely different without the Jews.

London in the thirties was, *pace* Mendelsohn and Taut, restive not restful. The aim has been to close Mendelsohn's perceived gap and re-present modern British architecture in terms of the exigencies of its cultural context, restoring to this material, by way of Highpoint II, the complexity it deserves, and to Mendelsohn's interregnum, an overlooked fullness. Through Lubetkin, we see the weight of the avant-garde emerging in classical caryatids instead of modernist *pilotis*, the weight of the future as London aimed to reconstruct itself after wartime damage, the weight of history, and the weight of his hidden Jewish identity.

That, concrete canopy aside, is a huge load to carry.

Notes

1 Warburton, *Ernö Goldfinger*, 70.
2 Louise Kehoe, http://lilith.org/articles/louise-kehoe-converts-why/, 1996. On file with author.
3 Louise Kehoe, *In this Dark House* (New York: Penguin, 1995), 229.
4 Allan's biography of Lubetkin was published before Kehoe corrected the record.
5 Kehoe, *In this Dark House*, 229.
6 Hitchcock, "L'Architecture Contemporaine en Angleterre," 443–6.
7 Kathryn Morrison and John Minnis, *Carscapes: The Motor Car, Architecture and Landscape in England* (London: Paul Mellon Centre for Studies in British Art, 2012), 258.
8 Erwin Panofsky, "The Ideological Antecedents of the Rolls-Royce Radiator" (1962) in Irving Lavin, ed., *Three Essays on Style* (Cambridge, MA: The MIT Press, 1997), 129–36. As a relevant side note to this discussion of "remaining quiet," Panofsky and the American writer Booth Tarkington exchanged a series of letters with each other for a period of eight years, from 1938 to 1946. By that time, Panofsky was settled in Princeton, New Jersey, far from the events of World War II. In a 1944 exchange, Tarkington belittled Panofsky's evident distress at having been on the receiving end of an anti-Semitic slight, treating it as unimportant and not worth mulling over. In Panofsky's reply, it is heartbreakingly clear he has been shamed into taking Tarkington's advice and chastises himself for even caring. See Richard M. Ludwig, ed., *Dr. Panofsky and Mr. Tarkington: An Exchange of Letters 1938–1946* (Princeton: Princeton University Library, 1974), 44–59.
9 Harries, *Nikolaus Pevsner*, 443. Banham's accusation can be found in his essay, "Revenge of the Picturesque: English Architectural Polemics, 1945–1965," in John Summerson, ed., *Concerning Architecture: Essays on Architectural Writers and Writing presented to Nikolaus Pevsner* (London: Allen Lane/The Penguin Press, 1968), 265. Michela Rosso has considered English modern architecture in terms of a dichotomy, where radical thought is always tempered by an inseparability from "traditionalism." See her essay "John N. Summerson and the Tales of Modern Architecture," *The Journal of Architecture* 5 (Spring 2000): 65–89. Some issues relating to Pevsner and nationalism are addressed in Peter Draper, ed., *Reassessing Nikolaus Pevsner* (London: Routledge, 2004).
10 The latter phrase is Meyer Schapiro's, quoted by Kuspit. Kuspit's lyrical exploration of the inherent Jewishness in the writing of Bernard Berenson, Meyer Schapiro, Clement Greenberg, and Harold Rosenberg and his ultimate conclusion that there is a particular sort of Jewish artisticness that stems from one's outsider status in society can be found in Kuspit, "Meyer Schapiro's Jewish Unconscious," in Catherine M. Soussloff, ed., *Jewish Identity in Modern Art History* (Berkeley and Los Angeles: UCLA Press, 1999), 200–17. Kuspit's essay was originally published in 1996.
11 Alan Powers, "Peter Moro: Obituary," *Independent* (October 20, 1998).

12 Glendinning and Muthesius, *Tower Block*, 127.

13 Fredric Bedoire, *The Jewish Contribution to Modern Architecture, 1830–1930* (New Jersey: KTAV Publishing House, in collaboration with Stockholm: Paideia and Kungliga Konsthögskolan, 2004), 507.

14 Esther da Costa Meyer, "Pierre Chareau: A Life Interrupted," in da Costa Meyer, ed., *Pierre Chareau: Modern Architecture and Design* (New York: The Jewish Museum and New Haven: Yale University Press, 2016), 14–39. Da Costa Meyer does imply that scholars need to make closer consideration of Chareau's Jewish roots. His wife Dollie strongly identified as Jewish, though Chareau did not.

15 Lara Trubowitz, *Civil Antisemitism, Modernism, and British Culture, 1902–1939* (New York: Palgrave Macmillan, 2012).

16 Sibyl Moholy-Nagy, "The Diaspora," *Journal of the Society of Architectural Historians* 24 (March 1965): 24; this is a special issue of *JSAH* devoted to the thirties, based on the Columbia proceedings.

17 Edward Said, "Reflections on Exile," in Russell Ferguson, Martha Gever, Trinh T. Minh-ha, et al., eds., *Out There: Marginalization and Contemporary Cultures* (New York and Cambridge, MA: The New Museum of Contemporary Art/The MIT Press, 1990), 357.

18 Tafuri and Dal Co, *Modern Architecture*, 257. The term "diaspora" is used in Italian as well; see Tafuri and Dal Co, *Architettura Contemporanea* (Venezia: Electra Editrice, 1976), 256. William Curtis refers to Lubetkin as a diaspora architect and discerns what he calls a "schizophrenia" in his work from being torn between two cultures, but he does not give any examples that explain what he means. See Curtis, "Berthold Lubetkin, or 'Socialist' Architecture in the Diaspora."

19 Mumford, *The CIAM Discourse on Urbanism*, 117. This sense continued into the postwar period; in a 1951 BBC radio address, Le Corbusier praised England for giving its young architects the chance to have large commissions, noting that France was simply not as generous; see "Le Corbusier Parle . . . 1951," an English translation of the transcription of his French speech, trans. Emmanuelle Morgan, in Elain Harwood and Alan Powers, eds., *Festival of Britain*, special issue of the journal of *Twentieth Century Architecture* 5 (London, 2001): 9–10.

20 Carol Zemel, *Looking Jewish: Visual Culture and Modern Diaspora* (Indianapolis: Indiana University Press, 2015). Detailed theorizations regarding exile and diaspora culture are out of the scope of this study. The literature on these topics is vast, wide-ranging, and disparate in view. For summaries of some of the scholarship see Deborah Lewittes, "London Calling: Modern Architecture in the Diaspora, 1933–51" (Ph.D. diss., City University of New York Graduate School and University Center, 2003).

21 Ian Fleming, *Goldfinger* (London: Jonathan Cape, 1959). The story surrounding Fleming's relationship to Goldfinger and his wife is taken up in Warburton, *Ernö Goldfinger*, 1–3. The foreign-born modern architect working in London appears as a character type in Michael Frayn, *Benefactors* (London: Methuen, 1991 [1984]), 60. The play follows a modernist, "rarefied Hampstead architect[s] of foreign extraction" forced to yield his ideals. The general Hampstead area indeed is where many foreign artists and intellectuals settled, and where the Highpoints, Lawn Road Flats, and Goldfinger's Willow Road home are all located.

22 Carter and Goldfinger, *The County of London Plan Explained*, 5.

23 Alison Smithson, ed., *Team Ten Primer* (Cambridge, MA: The MIT Press, 1968), 75.

24 See for instance Jonathan Hughes and Simon Sadler, eds., *Non-Plan: Essays on Freedom, Participation, and Change in Modern Architecture and Urbanism* (Oxford and Boston: Architectural Press, 2000), which focuses on the participatory discourse of much post-sixties avant-garde practice, often seen as a reaction against the English Welfare State.

25 Goldfinger, "The Sensation of Space," *The Architectural Review* 90 (November 1941): 129–31; "Urbanism and Spatial Order," *The Architectural Review* 90 (December 1941): 163–6; "Elements of Enclosed Space," *The Architectural Review* 91 (January 1942): 5–8. The essays are reprinted in James Dunnett and Gavin Stamp, *Ernö Goldfinger* (London: AA, 1983); "Sensation," 47–50; "Urbanism," 51–4; "Elements," 55–8. Citations are from the Dunnett and Stamp reprints.

26 Goldfinger, "Sensation of Space," 47. Emphasis original.

27 Warburton, *Ernö Goldfinger*, 94.

28 Stanley Tigerman, *The Architecture of Exile* (New York: Rizzoli International Publications, 1988). The anthropologist James A. Boon has criticized Said for mystifying this sense of cultural "outsider-ness." See Boon, *Affinities and Extremes: Crisscrossing the Bittersweet Ethnology of East Indies History, Hindu-Balinese Culture, and Indo-European Allure* (Chicago: University of Chicago Press, 1990), 210–11n.1. Recent interest in exploring links between Jewishness and the arts include Rose-Carol Washton Long, Matthew Baigell, et al., eds., *Jewish Dimensions in Modern Visual Culture* (Waltham, MA: Brandeis University Press, 2010).

Selected bibliography

Archival sources
British Architectural Library, Royal Institute of British Architects (RIBA), London
Selected papers:

ArO   Papers of Ove Arup

CaE   Papers of E.J. Carter

F&D   Papers of Maxwell Fry and Jane Drew

GoEr   Papers of Ernö Goldfinger

LuB   Papers of Berthold Lubetkin

MARS   Papers of The MARS Group

SaG   Papers of Godfrey Samuel

TyJ   Papers of Jaquelyn Tyrwhitt

AASTA (Association of Architects, Surveyors and Technical Assistants). *A.R.P.: A Report on the Design, Equipment and Cost of Air-Raid Shelters*. London: The Architects' Journal 1938. Includes foreword by The A.R.P. Committee and reprint of article from *The Architects' Journal* 88 (July 7, 1938).

Abercrombie, Patrick and J.H. Forshaw. *County of London Plan*. London: Macmillan and Co., 1943.

Abram, Joseph. "Ernö Goldfinger 1902–1987." *L'architecture d'aujourd'hui* 256 (April 1988): 61–2.

Aitken, Keith. Letter to the editor. *The Architects' Journal* 81 (1935): 159–60.

Allan, John. *Berthold Lubetkin: Architecture and the Tradition of Progress*. London: RIBA, 1992.

Allan, John. *Berthold Lubetkin*. London: Merrell, 2002.

Anderson, Stanford. "Modern Architecture and Industry: Peter Behrens, the AEG, and Industrial Design." *Oppositions* 21 (Summer 1980): 53–83.

AR 30s. Special issue of *The Architectural Review* 166 (November 1979).

"Architects' Refugee Relief Fund" and other letters to the editor. *Journal of the Royal Institute of British Architects* 46 (June 26, 1939): 830–1.

"A.R.P." *Journal of the Royal Institute of British Architects* 46 (January 9, 1939): 238–41.

"A.R.P. Handbook No. 5." Review of *Air Raid Precautions Handbook No. 5. Structural Defence. Journal of the Royal Institute of British Architects* 46 (June 26, 1939): 834–5.

Arts Council of Great Britain. *Le Corbusier: Architect of the Century.* London: Hayward Gallery, 1987.

Arup, Ove. "The Engineer Looks Back: Arup Associations." *AR 30s,* special issue of *The Architectural Review* 166 (November 1979): 315–21.

Aslan, N.J. "City." *The Architects' Journal* 98 (December 9, 1943): 429–32.

ATO (Architects' and Technicians' Organization). *ATO Bulletin* 1 (May 1936).

Augur, Tracy B. "The Dispersal of Cities as a Defense Measure." *Journal of the American Institute of Planners* 14 no. 3 (Summer 1948): 29–35.

Aulich, James and John Lynch, eds. *Critical Kitaj: Essays on the Work of R.B. Kitaj.* New Brunswick: Rutgers University Press, 2001.

Ayer, A.J. *The Foundations of Empirical Knowledge.* London: Macmillan & Co., 1940.

Ayer, A.J. *Language, Truth and Logic.* New York: Dover Publications, Inc., 1946 (1936).

Banham, Reyner. "Façade: Elevational Treatment of the Hallfield Estate Paddington." *The Architectural Review* 116 (November 1954): 302–7.

Banham, Reyner. "The New Brutalism." *The Architectural Review* 118 (December 1955): 354–61.

Banham, Reyner. *The New Brutalism: Ethic or Aesthetic?.* New York: Reinhold Publishing Corporation, 1966.

Banham, Reyner. *Theory and Design in the First Machine Age.* Cambridge, MA: The MIT Press, 1960.

Barron, Stephanie, ed. *"Degenerate Art": The Fate of the Avant-Garde in Nazi Germany.* New York: Harry N. Abrams, Inc., 1991.

Barron, Stephanie, ed. *Exiles and Émigrés: The Flight of European Artists from Hitler.* New York: Harry N. Abrams, Inc., 1997.

"Bassin des pingouins dans le zoo de Londres." *L'architecture d'aujourd'hui* 5 (September 1934): 60–2.

Bauer, Catherine. *Modern Housing.* London: Allen & Unwin, 1935 (American edition, 1934).

Beck, Haig, ed. *The State of the Art: A Cultural History of British Architecture.* Special issue of UIA-International Architect. London: International Architect Publishing Ltd., 1984.

Bedoire, Fredric. *The Jewish Contribution to Modern Architecture 1830–1930.* New Jersey: KTAV Publishing House, in collaboration with Stockholm: Paideia and Kungliga Konsthögskolan, 2004.

Behr, Shulamith and Marian Malet, eds. *Arts in Exile in Britain 1933–1945: Politics and Cultural Identity*. London: University of London/Rodopi, 2004.

Bennett, T.P. "Flats." *The Architect and Building News* 157 (February 17, 1939): 220–1.

Benton, Charlotte. *A Different World: Émigré Architects in Britain 1928–1958*. London: RIBA Heinz Gallery, 1995.

Bernal, J.D. *The Social Function of Science*. London: George Routledge & Sons Ltd., 1944 (1939).

Bettley, James. "Godfrey Samuel, 1904–1982." *RIBA Transactions* 4 no. 1(7) (1984–5): 83–91.

Blomfield, Reginald. *Modernismus*. London: Macmillan and Co., 1934.

Bolchover, Richard. *British Jewry and the Holocaust*. Oxford: The Littman Library of Jewish Civilization, 2003.

Boon, James A. *Affinities and Extremes: Crisscrossing the Bittersweet Ethnology of East Indies History, Hindu-Balinese Culture, and Indo-European Allure*. Chicago: University of Chicago Press, 1990.

Bosman, Jos. "CIAM After the War: A Balance of the Modern Movement." *Rassegna* 52 (December 1992): 6–21.

Boyer, M. Christine. *Not Quite Architecture: Writing Around Alison and Peter Smithson*. Cambridge, MA: The MIT Press, 2017.

Branson, Noreen and Margot Heinemann. *Britain in the Nineteen-Thirties*. Part of the series *The History of British Society*, ed. Eric Hobsbawm. Frogmore: Panther Books, 1971.

Brett, Lionel. "Doubts on the MARS Plan for London." *The Architects' Journal* 96 (July 9, 1942): 23–5.

Brett, Lionel. "Failure of the New Towns." *The Architectural Review* 114 (August 1953): 119–20.

Brett, Lionel and Berthold Lubetkin, "Canons of Criticism: 2." *The Architectural Review* 109 (March 1951): 135–7.

Brown, Denise Scott. "Team 10, Perspecta 10, and the Present State of Architectural Theory." *American Institute of Planners* 33 (January 1967): 42–50.

Buchloh, Benjamin H.D. *Neo-Avantgarde and Culture Industry: Essays on European and American Art from 1955 to 1975*. Cambridge, MA and London: The MIT Press, 2000.

"Buildings Revisited: Lansbury, Poplar 1951." *The Architects' Journal* 160 (July 3, 1974): 23–41.

Bullock, Nicholas. "Ideals, Priorities and Harsh Realities: Reconstruction and the LCC, 1945–51." *Planning Perspectives* 9 no. 1 (January 1994): 87–101.

Bullock, Nicholas. "Plans for Post-War Housing in the UK: The Case for Mixed Development and the Flat." *Planning Perspectives* 2 no. 1 (January 1987): 71–98.

Burke, David. *The Lawn Road Flats: Spies, Writers, and Artists*. Woodbridge, UK and Rochester, NY: The Boydell Press, 2014.

Burke, David. *The Spy Who Came in from the Co-op: Melita Norwood and the Ending of Cold War Espionage*. Woodbridge: The Boydell Press, 2008.

Camp, D'Laine, Dirk van den Heuvel, and Gijs de Waal, eds. *Team 10: Between Modernity and the Everyday*. TU Delft, 2003.

Campbell, Louise. "Architecture and Client: Modern Architecture in Its Context, England 1919–39." Ph.D. diss., University of London, 1983.

Campbell, Louise. *Coventry Cathedral: Art and Architecture in Post-war Britain*. Oxford: Oxford University Press, 1996.

Campbell, Louise. "The MARS Group 1933–39." *RIBA Transactions* 4 no. 2(8) (1984–5): 68–79.

Campbell, Louise, ed. *Twentieth-Century Architecture and Its Histories*. Otley: Society of Architectural Historians of Great Britain, 2000.

Carey, Oliver and Charlotte. "Unité d'Habitation." *Architects' Year Book* 4 (1952): 131–6.

Carter, E.J. and Ernö Goldfinger. *The County of London Plan Explained*. London: Penguin, 1945.

Casson, Hugh. "The English Scene." *Architectural Record* 81 (March 1937): 7–10.

Causey, Andrew, ed. *Paul Nash: Writings on Art*. Oxford: Oxford University Press. 2000.

Chalk, Warren. Untitled essay on architecture in the nineteen-forties. *Archigram* 6 (Autumn 1965): unpaginated.

Chermayeff, Serge. "Architects and the AR.P." *Pencil Points* 21 (November 1940). Special supplement.

Chermayeff, Serge. "A.R.P. and Our Office of Civilian Defense." *Pencil Points* 22 (September 1941): 591–3.

Chermayeff, Serge and J.M. Richards. "A Hundred Years Ahead: Forecasting the Coming Century." *The Architects' Journal* 81 (January 10, 1935): 79–86.

Chippendale, I.[pseudo]. "The LCC Was Our Uncle." *Architectural Design* 35 (September 1965): 428.

Coates, Wells. "The Conditions for an Architecture for Today." *Arena: Architectural Association Journal* 53 (April 1938): 447–57.

Coe, Peter and Malcolm Reading. *Lubetkin and Tecton: Architecture and Social Commitment*. London: The Arts Council of Great Britain, 1981.

Cohn, Laura. *The Door to a Secret Room: A Portrait of Wells Coates*. Aldershot: Scolar Press; Brookfield, VT: Ashgate Publishing Co., 1999.

Colquhoun, A.I.T. "Twentieth-Century Picturesque." Letter to the editor, *The Architectural Review* 116 (July 1954): 2.

"A Concrete Garden City of the Future." *The Architect and Building News* 145 (March 27, 1936): 389–90.

Conekin, Becky, Frank Mort, and Chris Waters, eds. *Moments of Modernity: Reconstructing Britain 1945–1964*. London and New York: Rivers Oram Press/ New York University, 1999.

Conrads, Ulrich, ed. *Programs and Manifestoes on Twentieth-Century Architecture*. Translated by Michael Bullock. Cambridge, MA: The MIT Press, 1970.

Conway, Martin and Jose Gotovitch, eds. *Europe in Exile Communities in Britain 1940–1945*. New York: Berghahn Books, 2001.

Cook, Peter. "Situation: England 1965." *Archigram* 6 (Autumn 1965): unpaginated.

Cooke, Catherine. *Russian Avant-Garde: Theories of Art, Architecture, and the City*. London: Academy Editions, 1995.

Corbett, David Peters. *The Modernity of English Art 1914–30*. Manchester and New York: Manchester University Press, 1997.

Corbett, David Peters and Lara Perry. *English Art 1860–1914: Modern Artists and Identity*. Manchester: Manchester University Press, 2000 and New Brunswick: Rutgers University Press, 2001.

Corbett, David Peters, Ysanne Holt, and Fiona Russell, eds. *The Geographies of Englishness: Landscape and the National Past, 1880–1940*. New Haven and London: Yale University Press, 2002.

Cormier, Leslie Humm. "Walter Gropius: Émigré Architect." Ph.D. diss., Brown University, 1986.

"The County of London Plan." *The Architect and Building News* 175 (July 16, 1943): 29–32.

Le Corbusier. "The MARS Group Exhibition of the Elements of Modern Architecture." Translated by P.M.S. [P. Morton Shand]. *The Architectural Review* 83 (March 1938): 109–10.

Le Corbusier. *Towards a New Architecture*. Translated by Frederick Etchells. New York: Dover Publications, Inc., 1931 (French edition, 1923).

Le Corbusier. "The Vertical Garden City." *The Architectural Review* 79 (January 1936): 9–10.

Cox, Anthony. "Highpoint II, North Hill, Highgate." *Focus* 2 (Winter 1948): 71–9.

Cox, Anthony and Leo DeSyllas. "CIAM Congress, 1947." *Plan* 1 (1948): 13–17.

Crompton, Richmal. *William and A.R.P.* London: George Newnes, 1939.

Curtis, William. "Berthold Lubetkin, or 'Socialist' Architecture in the Diaspora." *AAQ (Architectural Association Quarterly)* 8 no. 3 (1976): 33–9.

Curtis, William. *English Architecture 1930s: The Modern Movement in England 1930–9; Thoughts on the Political Content and Associations of the International Style*. Milton Keynes: The Open University Press, 1975.

Curtis, William. *Modern Architecture Since 1900*. London: Phaidon, 1996.

da Costa Meyer, Esther, ed. *Pierre Chareau: Modern Architecture and Design*. New York: The Jewish Museum; New Haven: Yale University Press, 2016.

Dannatt, Trevor. *Modern Architecture in Britain*. With an introduction by John Summerson. London: Arts Council of Great Britain, 1959.

Davis, Richard Llewelyn. "Endless Architecture." *AAJ (Architectural Association Journal)* 67 (November 1951): 106–13.

Dean, David. *The Thirties: Recalling the English Architectural Scene*. London: Trefoil Books, 1983.

"The Decade 1929–39." Special issue of *Journal of the Society of Architectural Historians* 24 (March 1965).

"Decentralisation and Town Growth: The Problem of the Industrial Expansion of London." Review of a pamphlet by the same title published by the Garden Cities and Town Planning Association, *Journal of the Town Planning Institute* 14 (September 1928): 258–9.

de Maré, Eric. "The New Empiricism: The Antecedents and Origins of Sweden's Latest Style." *The Architectural Review* 103 (January 1948): 9–22.

Denby, Elizabeth. "The All-Europe House." *Journal of the Royal Institute of British Architects* 46 (June 26, 1939): 813–19.

Denby, Elizabeth. *Europe Re-housed*. London: George Allen & Unwin Ltd., 1938.

de Wofle [*sic*], Ivor [Hugh de Cronin Hastings], ed. *The Architectural Review* 154 (October 1973). Special issue on new towns.

de Wolfe, I. [Hugh de Cronin Hastings]. "Townscape: A Plea for an English Visual Philosophy Founded on the True Rock of Sir Uvedale Price." *The Architectural Review* 106 (December 1949): 355–62. Followed by Gordon Cullen's "Townscape Casebook," 363–74.

Diehl, Thomas. "Theory and Principle: Berthold Lubetkin's Highpoint One and Highpoint Two." *Journal of Architectural Education* 4 (May 1999): 233–41.

Draper, Peter, ed. *Reassessing Nikolaus Pevsner*. London: Routledge, 2004.

Dunnett, James and Gavin Stamp. *Ernö Goldfinger*. London: AA, 1983.

Durant, Ruth. *Watling: A Survey of Social Life on a New Estate*. London: S. King and Son, Ltd., 1939.

Eisenman, Peter. "From Golden Lane to Robin Hood Gardens: Or If You Follow the Yellow Brick Road, It May Not Lead to Golders Green." *Oppositions* 1 (September 1973): 27–56. Reprinted in Eisenman, *Inside Out: Selected Writings 1963–1988*. New Haven: Yale University Press, 2004, 40–56.

"Elizabeth Denby's 'All-Europe' House." *The Architect and Building News* (March 11, 1939): 319.

Elwall, Robert. *Building a Better Tomorrow: Architecture in Britain in the 1950s*. London: Wiley & Sons/RIBA, 2000.

Elwall, Robert. *Ernö Goldfinger*. London: Academy Editions, 1996.

Ernö Goldfinger, 1924–62. Special issue of *Architectural Design* 33 (January 1963).

Esau, Robert Jonathan. "Connell, Ward and Lucas and the Emergence of the British Modern Movement in Architecture." Ph.D. diss., Bryn Mawr College, 1994.

Esher, Lionel. *A Broken Wave: The Rebuilding of England, 1940–80*. London: Allen Lane, 1981.

"Europe Discusses the House." *The Architectural Review* 64 (December 1928): 221–30.

E.W. "Two Notes on the Cult of Ruins." Part I, "Ruins and Echoes"; Part II "Utopian Ruins," *Journal of the Warburg Institute* 1 (1937–8): 259–60.

"Exposition du 'Werkbund' à Stuttgart l'habitation." *Cahiers d'Art* 2 (1927): 287–92.

Felton, Monica. "Britain's Model New Industrial Town: Peterlee." *Journal of the American Institute of Planners* 15 no. 1 (Spring 1949): 40–3.

Ferguson, Russell, Martha Gever, Trinh T. Minh-ha, and Cornel West, eds. *Out There: Marginalization and Contemporary Cultures*. New York and Cambridge, MA: The New Museum of Contemporary Art/The MIT Press, 1990.

Fleming, Ian. *Goldfinger*. London: Jonathan Cape, 1959.

Frampton, Kenneth. "MARS and Beyond: The British Contribution to Modern Architecture." Review of *The Politics of Architecture: A History of Modern Architecture in Britain*, by Anthony Jackson. *AAQ (Architectural Association Quarterly)* 2 (October 1970): 51–5.

Frampton, Kenneth. *Modern Architecture: A Critical History*. London: Thames & Hudson, 2007.

Frampton, Kenneth. *Studies in Tectonic Culture*. Cambridge, MA: The MIT Press, 1995.

Frampton, Kenneth. "Towards a Critical Regionalism: Six Points for an Architecture of Resistance." In *The Anti-Aesthetic: Essays on Postmodern Culture*, edited by Hal Foster. Port Townsend, WA: The Bay Press, 1983.

Frayn, Michael. *Benefactors*. London: Methuen, 1991 (1984).

Fry, Maxwell. *Fine Building*. London: Faber & Faber, 1944.

Fry, Maxwell. "The Small House of Today." Review of *The Modern House*, by F.R.S. Yorke. *The Architectural Review* 76 (July 1934): 20.

Furneaux-Jordan, Robert. "Lubetkin." *The Architectural Review* 118 (July 1955): 36–44.

Galison, Peter. "Aufbau/Bauhaus: Logical Positivism and Architectural Modernism." *Critical Inquiry* 16 no. 4 (Summer 1990): 709–52.

"A Garden City of the Future: Designed by F.R.S. Yorke and Marcel Breuer." *The Architects' Journal* 83 (March 26, 1936): 477–82.

Garlake, Margaret. "The Construction of National Identity at the 1951 Festival of Britain." *AICARC: Bulletin of the Archives and Documentation Centers for Modern and Contemporary Art* (Zurich) 1&2 nos. 29–30 (1991): 16–20.

Garlake, Margaret. *New Art, New World: British Art in Postwar Society*. New Haven and London: Yale University Press, 1998.

Getsy, David. "Locating Modern Art in Britain." *Art Journal* (Winter 2001): 98–102.

Gibberd, Frederick. "Expression in Modern Architecture." *Journal of the Royal Institute of British Architects* 59 (January 1952): 79–87.

Gibberd, Frederick. "Three Dimensional Aspects of Housing Layout." *Journal of the Royal Institute of British Architects* 55 (August 1948): 433–40.

Giedion, Sigfried. *Space, Time and Architecture: The Growth of a New Tradition*, 4th edn. Cambridge, MA: The MIT Press, 1963 (1941).

Giedion, Sigfried. *Walter Gropius: Work and Teamwork*. New York: Reinhold Publishing Corporation, 1954.

Glass, Ruth. "Social Aspects of Town-Planning." *The Architects' Journal* 100 (October 26, 1944): 306–7.

Glendinning, Miles and Stefan Muthesius, *Tower Block: Modern Public Housing in England, Scotland, Wales and Northern Ireland*. New Haven and London: The Paul Mellon Centre for Studies in British Art and Yale University Press, 1994.

Golan, Romy. "A 'Discours aux Architectes'?" *Rivista de Arquitectura* 5 (June 2003): 115–30.

Golan, Romy. "The 'École Française' vs. the 'École de Paris': The Debate about Artists in Paris Between the Wars." In *The Circle of Montparnasse: Jewish Artists in Paris 1905–1945*, edited by Kenneth E. Silver and Golan, 81–7. New York: The Jewish Museum/Universe Books, 1985.

Gold, John. "'Commoditie, Firmenes and Delight': Modernism, the MARS Group's 'New Architecture' Exhibition (1938) and Imagery of the Urban Future." *Planning Perspectives* 8 (1993): 357–76.

Gold, John. *The Experience of Modernism: Modern Architects and the Future City 1928–1933*. New York and London: E&FN Spon, 1997.

Gold, John. "The MARS Plans for London, 1933–1942: Plurality and Experimentation in the City Plans of the Early British Modern Movement." *Town Planning Review* 66 no. 3 (July 1995): 243–67.

Gold, John and Stephen V. Ward, "Of Plans and Planners: Documentary Film and the Challenge of the Urban Future, 1935–52." In *The Cinematic City*, edited by David B. Clarke, 59–82. London: Routledge, 1997.

"Golden Lane Competition: A Selection of Unsuccessful Entries." *The Architects' Journal* 115 (March 20, 1952): 358–60.

Goldfinger, Ernö. "Architecture – the Art of Enclosing Space." *AAJ (Architectural Association Journal)* 63 (March 1948): 177–87.

Goldfinger, Ernö. "Elements of Enclosed Space." *The Architectural Review* 91 (January 1942): 5–8.

Goldfinger, Ernö. "For the Family: A House, a Flat … or Something Between the Two?" *The Ideal Home and Gardening* 46 no. 3 (September 1942): 128–31.

Goldfinger, Ernö, ed. *Grande-Bretagne*. Special issue of *L'architecture d'aujourd'hui* 39 (February 1952).

Goldfinger, Ernö. "The Sensation of Space." *The Architectural Review* 90 (November 1941): 129–31.

Goldfinger, Ernö. "Urbanism and Spatial Order." *The Architectural Review* 90 (December 1941): 163–6.

Goldhagen, Sarah and Réjean Legault, eds. *Anxious Modernisms: Experimentation in Postwar Architectural Culture*. Cambridge, MA: The MIT Press; Montreal: The Canadian Centre for Architecture, 2000.

Goodhart-Rendel, H.S. "The Principles of Patchwork." Part IV of "London that Is to Be." *Country Life* (January 4, 1941): 4–6.

Goodhart-Rendel, H.S. "Professor Abercrombie Proposes." *Architect and Building News* 183 (September 28, 1945): 191–3.

Gowan, James, ed. *A Continuing Experiment: Learning and Teaching at the Architectural Association*. London: The Architectural Press, 1975.

Gray, Camilla. *The Great Experiment: Russian Art 1863–1922*. London: Thames & Hudson, 1962.

"A Guide to Postwar London." *Architectural Design* 31 (June 1961): 232ff.

Haldane, J.B.S. *A.R.P.* London: Victor Gollancz Ltd., 1938.

Haldane, J.B.S. "A.R.P.: The Informal Meeting on 14 December." *Journal of the Royal Institute of British Architects* 46 (January 9, 1939): 238.

Haldane, J.B.S. *How to Be Safe from Air Raids*. London: Victor Gollancz Ltd., 1938.

Haldane, J.B.S. "The Mathematics of Air Raid Protection." *Journal of the Royal Institute of British Architects* 46 (January 9, 1939): 240–1.

Haldane, J.B.S. *Possible Worlds and Other Essays*. London: Chatto & Windus, 1930 (1927).

Hamilton, P.T. "The Role of Futurism, Dada, and Surrealism in the Construction of British Modernism 1910–1940." Ph.D. diss., University of Oxford, 1987.

Hampstead in the Thirties. London: Camden Arts Centre, 1974.

Harries, Susan. *Nikolaus Pevsner: The Life*. London: Chatto & Windus, 2011.

Harris, G. Montagu. "Town Planning, City Planning, Urbanisme and Städtebau." *Journal of the Town Planning Institute* 14 (May 1928): 151–6.

Harrison, Charles. *English Art and Modernism 1900–39.* London: Allen Lane; Bloomington: Indiana University Press, 1981.

Harrisson, Tom. *Britain Revisited.* London: Victor Gollancz Ltd., 1961.

Harrisson, Tom. *The Journey Home.* Mass Observation. London: John Murray, 1944.

Harrisson, Tom and Charles Madge, eds. *War Begins at Home.* Mass Observation. London: Chatto & Windus/Mass Observation, 1940.

Harwood, Elain and Alan Powers, eds. *Festival of Britain.* Special issue of *Twentieth-Century Architecture: Journal of the Twentieth-Century Society* 5 (2001).

Hawkins, J. and M. Hollis, eds. *The Thirties: British Art and Design before the War.* London: Arts Council of Great Britain, 1979.

Hewison, Robert. *Under Siege: Literary Life in London 1939–45.* Exeter: A. Wheaton and Co., Ltd./Readers Union, 1977.

Hitchcock, Henry-Russell. "The Architecture of Bureaucracy and the Architecture of Genius." *The Architectural Review* 101 (January 1947): 3–6.

Hitchcock, Henry-Russell. "L'Architecture Contemporaine en Angleterre." *Cahiers d'art* (1928): 443–6.

Hitchcock, Henry-Russell. "England and the Outside World." *Architectural Association Journal* 72 (November 1956): 96–7.

Hitchcock, Henry-Russell and Philip Johnson. *The International Style.* New York and London: W.W. Norton, 1966 (1932).

Holz, Keith. *Modern German Art for Thirties Paris, Prague, and London.* Ann Arbor: University of Michigan Press, 2004.

"Housing: Bethnal Green, London." *The Architectural Review* 127 (May 1960): 304–12.

Hughes, Jonathan and Simon Sadler, eds. *Non-Plan: Essays on Freedom Participation and Change in Modern Architecture and Urbanism.* Oxford and Boston: The Architectural Press, 2000.

Huxley, Julian. "Science and the House." *Plan* 3 (1945): 14–16.

Huxley, Julian. *Scientific Research and Social Needs.* London: Watts and Co., 1934.

Institut français d'architecture. *Berthold Lubetkin, un moderne en Angleterre.* Liège: Pierre Mardaga, 1983.

Jackson, Anthony. *The Politics of Architecture: A History of Modern Architecture in Britain.* London: The Architectural Press, 1970.

Jackson, Anthony. "Politics of Architecture: English Architecture 1929–51." *Journal of the Society of Architectural Historians* 24 (1965): 97–107.

Jackson, W. Eric. *Achievement: A Short History of the LCC.* London: Longman Green and Co., 1965.

Jeffcott, Ian. "Thoughts on the Function of the Building Exhibition." *The Architectural Review* 16 (August 1934): 75–6.

Johnson-Marshall, Percy. *Rebuilding Cities.* With an introduction by Lewis Mumford. Edinburgh: Edinburgh University Press, 1966.

Jordy, William H. "The Symbolic Essence of Modern European Architecture of the Twenties and Its Continuing Influence." *Journal of the Society of Architectural Historians* 22 (1963): 177–87.

Keay, L.H. "Are Working Class Flats a Solution of the Problem of Rehousing?" *Town and Country Planning* 3 no. 1 (December 1934): 92–4.

Kehoe, Louise. *In This Dark House.* New York: Penguin, 1995.

Kehoe, Louise. http://lilith.org/articles/louise-kehoe-converts-why/, 1996. On file with author.

"Kensal House." *Journal of the Royal Institute of British Architects* 44 (March 20, 1937): 500–5.

"Kensal House, Ladbroke Grove." *The Architect and Building News* 149 (March 26, 1937): 380–4.

Kinoshita, Toshiko and Kenji Watanabe. "English Modern Houses in the 30s." Translated by Lewis Cook. Four-part article. *A+U* 322 (July 1997): 138–41; 324 (September 1997): 4–8; 327 (December 1997): 132–6; 330 (March 1998): 102–7.

Kinross, Robin. "Émigré Graphic Designers in Britain: Around the Second World War and Afterwards." *Journal of Design History* 3 no. 1 (1990): 35–57.

Kirkham, Pat and David Thoms, eds. *War Culture: Social Change and Changing Experience in World War II.* London: Lawrence & Wishart, 1995.

Kopp, Anatole. "Émigration des architectes. Architecture de l'émigration." In *Quand le moderne n'était pas un style mais une cause.* Paris: École nationale supérieure des Beaux-Arts, 1988.

Korn, Arthur. *History Builds the Town.* London: Lund Humphries, 1955.

Korn, Arthur. "The MARS Plan for London." *Perspecta* 13/14 (1971): 164.

Korn, Arthur and Felix J. Samuely. "A Master Plan for London Based on Research Carried Out by the Town Planning Committee of the M.A.R.S. Group." *The Architectural Review* 91 (June 1942): 143–50.

Kunst im Exil in Grossbritannien 1933–1945. Exh. Cat., Neue Gesellschaft für Bildende Kunst, Berlin. Berlin: Frölich & Kaufmann/NGBK, 1986.

Landau, Royston. "The End of CIAM and the Role of the British." *Rassegna* 52 (December 1992): 40–7.

Landau, Royston. *New Directions in British Architecture.* New York: George Braziller, 1968.

Lasdun, Denys. "Second Thoughts on Housing in London." *Architects' Year Book* 4 (1952): 137–8.

"The Last CIAMs." Special issue of *Rassegna* 52 (December 1992).

"LCC Housing." *The Architects' Journal* 109 (May 26, 1949): 474–83.

Lewison, Jeremy, ed. *Circle: Constructive Art in Britain 1934–40.* Cambridge: Kettle's Yard Gallery, 1982.

Lewittes, Deborah. "London Calling: Modern Architecture in the Diaspora, 1933–51." Ph.D. diss., City University of New York Graduate School and University Center, 2003.

Lipstadt, Hélène. "Polemic and Parody in the Battle for British Modernism." *Oxford Art Journal* 5 (1983): 22–30.

Lodder, Christina. *Russian Constructivism.* New Haven and London: Yale University Press, 1983.

London, Louise. *Whitehall and the Jews, 1933–1948: British Immigration Policy, Jewish Refugees and the Holocaust.* Cambridge: Cambridge University Press, 2000.

"London that Is to Be." Four-part series in *Country Life*. Charles Bressey (November 23, 1940): 446–7; Gwilym Gibbey (December 7, 1940): 497; Thomas Sharp (December 21, 1940): 536–7; H.S. Goodhart-Rendel (January 4, 1941): 4–6.

Long, Rose-Carol Washton, Matthew Baigell, and Milly Heyd, eds. *Jewish Dimensions in Modern Visual Culture*. Waltham, MA: Brandeis University Press, 2010.

Lubetkin, Berthold. "L'architecture en Angleterre." *L'architecture d'aujourd'hui* 3ième année 2 ième ser. No. 10 (December 1932–January 1933): 3–23.

Lubetkin, Berthold. "A Block of Flats in Paris." *The Architectural Review* 73 (1932): 135–8.

Lubetkin, Berthold. "The Builders." Two-part article. Part I: "Architectural Thought since the Revolution," 201–3. Part 2: "Recent Developments of Town Planning in U.S.S.R.," 209–16. *The Architectural Review* 71 (May 1932), special issue entitled "The Russian Scene."

Lubetkin, Berthold. "Flats in Holford Square, Finsbury." *The Architectural Review* 111 (June 1952): 403–6.

Lubetkin, Berthold. "Flats in Rosebery Avenue, Finsbury." *The Architectural Review* 109 (March 1951): 138–50.

Lubetkin, Berthold. "Modern Architecture in England." *American Architect and Architecture* 150 (February 1937): 29–42.

Lubetkin, Berthold. "President's Invitation Lecture." *RIBA Transactions* 4 no. 2(8) (1984–5): 5–11.

Lubetkin, Berthold. "Soviet Architecture: Notes on Developments from 1917–1932." *Architectural Association Journal* 71 (1956): 260–4.

Lubetkin, Berthold. "Soviet Architecture: Notes on Developments from 1932–1955." *Architectural Association Journal* 72 (1956): 85–7.

Lubetkin, Berthold. "Town and Landscape Planning in Soviet Russia." *AA Journal* (January 1933): 186–201.

Lubetkin, Berthold and F.R.S. Yorke. "The Russian Aesthetic." *The Architectural Review* 11 (May 1932): 193–200.

Ludwig, Richard M., ed. *Dr. Panofsky and Mr. Tarkington: An Exchange of Letters 1938–1946*. Princeton: Princeton University Library, 1974.

Lycett, Andrew. *Ian Fleming*. London: Phoenix, 1995.

MacDougall, Sarah and Rachel Dickson. *Forced Journeys: Artists in Exile c. 1933–45*. London: The London Jewish Museum of Art, 2009.

MacQuedy, James [J.M. Richards]. Untitled piece on "The man in the street." *The Architectural Review* 87 (May 1940): 183–4.

Madge, John, ed. *Tomorrow's Houses: New Building Methods, Structures and Materials*. London: Pilot Press Limited, 1946.

Maguire, Patrick J. and Jonathan M. Woodham, eds. *Design and Cultural Politics in Postwar Britain: The Britain Can Make It Exhibition of 1946*. Leicester and Washington: Leicester University Press, 1997.

Marmaras, Emmanuel and Anthony Sutcliffe. "Planning for Post-war London: The Three Independent Plans, 1942–3." *Planning Perspectives* 9 no. 4 (October 1994): 431–53.

"The MARS Exhibition." Reviewed by students in Unit 15 of the AA School. *The Architectural Association Journal* 53 (February 1938): 386–8.

"The MARS Group." Series of letters to the editor. *The Architects' Journal* (May 10, 1933): 623.

Martian [pseudo.]. *A.R.P.: A Reply to Professor J.B.S. Haldane, the Royal institute of British Architects, and Some Others, Including the British Government.* London: John Bale, Sons & Curnow, Ltd., 1938.

Martin, J.L. "The Royal Festival Hall." *The Architects' Year Book* 4 (1952): 188–215.

Martin, J.L., Ben Nicholson, and N. Gabo. *Circle: International Survey of Constructive Art.* London: Faber & Faber, 1971 (1937).

Massey, Anne. *The Independent Group: Modernism and Mass Culture in Britain, 1945–59.* Manchester and New York: Manchester University Press, 1995.

Masters, David. "Constructions of National Identity: British Art 1930–1990." Ph.D. diss., Open University, 1996.

Maxwell, Robert. *New British Architecture.* New York: Praeger Publishers, 1972.

McGrath, Raymond. *Twentieth-Century Houses.* London: Faber & Faber, 1934.

McLeod, Mary. "Urbanism and Utopia: Le Corbusier from Regional Syndicalism to Vichy." Ph.D. diss., Princeton University, 1985.

Mellor, David. "Existentialism and Postwar British Art." In *Paris Postwar: Art and Existentialism,* edited by Frances Morris, 53–62. London: Tate Gallery, 1993.

Melvin, Jeremy and David Allford. "F.R.S. Yorke and 'The Modern House'." *Journal of the Twentieth-Century Society* 2 (1996): 28–40.

Mills, Edward D. *The New Architecture in Great Britain 1946–1953.* With a foreword by William Holford. New York: Reinhold Publishing Corporation; London: The Standard Catalogue Co., Ltd., 1953.

Ministry of Health. *Housing Manual.* London: HMSO, 1944.

Modern Architectural Research (MARS) Group. *New Architecture Exhibition: An Exhibition of the Elements of Modern Architecture Organized by the MARS Group.* London: New Burlington Galleries, 1938.

"Modern Flats at Hampstead." *The Architectural Review* 76 (July 1934): 77–82.

"Modern Flats in Highgate." *The Architectural Review* 84 (1938): 161–4.

Moffat, Isabelle. "'A horror of abstract thought': Postwar Britain and Hamilton's 1951 Growth and Form Exhibition." *October* 94 (Fall 2000): 89–112.

Moholy-Nagy, László. *The New Vision,* 4th edn. New York: Wittenborn, Schultz, Inc., 1947 (1928).

Moholy-Nagy, Sibyl. *Moholy-Nagy: Experiment in Totality.* With an introduction by Walter Gropius. Cambridge, MA: The MIT Press, 1950.

Moholy-Nagy, Sibyl. "The Diaspora." *Journal of the Society of Architectural Historians* 24 (March 1965): 24–5.

Moon, A.F.W. "The Garchey System of Refuse Disposal." *Architectural Design* 25 (September 1955): 298–9.

Morrison, Kathryn and John Minnis. *Carscapes: The Motor Car, Architecture and Landscape in England.* London: Paul Mellon Centre for Studies in British Art, 2012.

Mosse, Werner E., ed. *Second Chance: Two Centuries of German-speaking Jews in the United Kingdom.* Tübingen: J.C.B. Mohr, 1991.

Mowat, Charles Loeb. *Britain Between the Wars 1918–1940.* Chicago: University of Chicago Press, 1955.

Mowls, Timothy. *Stylistic Cold Wars: Betjeman vs. Pevsner.* London: John Murray, 2000.

Muggeridge, Malcolm. *The Thirties: 1930–40 in Great Britain.* London: Hamish Hamilton, 1940.

Mumford, Eric. *The CIAM Discourse on Urbanism, 1928–1960.* Cambridge, MA: The MIT Press, 2000.

Mumford, Eric. "CIAM Urbanism after the Athens Charter." *Planning Perspectives* 7 (1992): 391–417.

The Museum of Modern Art. *Modern Architecture in England.* New York: Arno Press, 1937.

Nairn, Ian. *Counter Attack Against Subtopia.* London: The Architectural Press, 1957.

Nairn, Ian, ed. "Outrage." Special issue of *The Architectural Review* 117 (June 1955).

Nash, Paul. "Going Modern and Being British." *The Weekend Review* (March 12, 1932): 322–3.

"National Housing and Town Planning Council: Strong Arguments for Decentralisation." *Town and Country Planning* 7 no. 26 (January–March 1939).

Nelson, George. "Architects of Europe Today, 12: Tecton." *Pencil Points* 17 (1936): 527–40.

"The New Empiricism: Sweden's Latest Style." *The Architectural Review* 101 (June 1947): 199–204.

"The New Homes for Old Housing Exhibit: The MARS Contribution." *The Architects' Journal* 80 (September 20, 1934): 425–7.

"The New R.I.B.A. Refugee Committee." *Journal of the Royal Institute of British Architects* 46 (February 6, 1939): 324.

Ockman, Joan. "New Empiricism and the New Humanism." *Design Book Review* 41/42 (Winter 2000): 18–21.

Ockman, Joan. "Toward a Theory of Normative Architecture." In *Architecture of the Everyday*, edited by Steven Harris and Deborah Berke, 122–52. New York: Princeton Architectural Press, 1997.

Ockman, Joan and Edward Eigen, eds. *Architecture Culture 1943–1968: A Documentary Anthology.* New York: Columbia Books of Architecture and Rizzoli International Publications, 1993.

Orwell, George. *England Your England and Other Essays.* London: Secker & Warburg, 1953.

Orwell, George. *The Lion and the Unicorn: Socialism and the English Genius.* London: Secker and Warburg, 1941.

Osborn, F.J. "Fantasies of Planning: The Tower and the Street." *Town and Country Planning* 5 no. 20 (September 1937): 119–21.

Panofsky, Erwin. "The Ideological Antecedents of the Rolls-Royce Radiator" (1962). In *Three Essays on Style*, edited by Irving Lavin, 129–36. Cambridge, MA: The MIT Press, 1997.

"Penguin Pond." *Architectural Record* 77 (February 1935): 107.

"Penguin Pond, Zoological Gardens." *The Architects' Journal* 19 (June 14, 1934): 856–9.

"The Penguin Pool in the Zoo." *The Architectural Review* 16 (July 1934): 17–19.

Perry, C.A. *Housing for the Machine Age*. New York: Russell Sage Foundation, 1939.

Peto, James and Donna Loveday, eds. *Modern Britain. 1929–39*. London: Design Museum, 1999.

Pevsner, Nikolaus. "English Architecture 1860–1930." *Architectural Record* 81 (March 1937): 1–6.

Pevsner, Nikolaus. *The Englishness of English Art*. Harmondsworth: Penguin, 1956.

Pevsner, Nikolaus. Letter to the editor. *The Architectural Review* 116 (July 1954): 2.

Pevsner, Nikolaus. *Pioneers of Modern Design: From William Morris to Walter Gropius*. New York: Penguin, 1975 (1936).

"Points from Papers: Peterlee New Town. Report of a talk by Dr. Monica Felton at the Housing Centre." *The Architect and Building News* 194 (November 12, 1948): 410–12.

Posener, Julius. "Knots in the Master's Carpet." *Architectural Design* 51 (December 1951): 356.

Powers, Alan. "C.H. Reilly: Regency, Englishness and Modernism." *Journal of Architecture* 5 (Spring 2000): 47–63.

Powers, Alan, ed. *H.S. Goodhart-Rendel 1887–1959*. London: The Architectural Association, 1987.

Powers, Alan. *In the Line of Development: F.R.S. Yorke, E. Rosenberg, and C.S. Mardell to YRM*. London: RIBA Heinz Gallery, 1992.

Powers, Alan. "Peter Moro: Obituary." *Independent* (October 20, 1998).

Powers, Alan. "The Re-conditioned Eye: Architects and Artists in English Modernism." *AA Files* 25 (Summer 1993): 54–62.

Powers, Alan. "A Zebra at Villa Savoye: Interpreting the Modern House." *Twentieth-Century Architecture: Journal of the Twentieth-Century Society* 2 (1996): 16–26.

Pritchard, Jack. *View from a Long Chair*. Boston and London: Routledge and Kegan Paul, 1984.

Rasmussen, Steen Eiler. *London, the Unique City*. London: Jonathan Cape, 1937. (Danish edition, 1934).

Ray, Paul C. *The Surrealist Movement in England*. Ithaca and London: Cornell University Press. 1971.

Read, Herbert. *Art Now: An Introduction to the Theory of Modern Painting and Sculpture*. London: Faber & Faber, 1933.

Read, Herbert. *The Meaning of Art*. London: Faber & Faber, 1931 (American edition, *The Anatomy of Art*).

Read, Herbert. "A Nest of Gentle Artists." *Apollo* 77 (September 1962): 536–42.

Read, Herbert, ed. *Unit One: The Modern Movement in English Architecture, Painting, and Sculpture*. London: Cassell and Company, Ltd., 1934.

Reading, Malcolm. "A History of the MARS Group 1933–45: A Thematic Analysis." DipArch thesis, The Architectural Association, 1986.

Reading, Malcolm. "Tall Order." *The Architects' Journal* 181 (June 5, 1985): 44–56.

Reading, Malcolm and Peter Coe. *Lubetkin & Tecton: An Architectural Study*. London: Triangle Architectural Publishing, 1992.

Remy, Michel. *Surrealism in Britain*. Brookfield, VT and Hants, England: Ashgate, 1999.

Richards, J.M. "Another Man's Poison." *The Architectural Review* 100 (December 1946): 153–6.

Richards, J.M. "The Architect and His Patrons." *Architectural Record* 81 (March 1937): 11–34.

Richards, J.M. "Architecture and the Common Man." *The Architects' Journal* 107 (February 5, 1948): 132–3.

Richards, J.M. "The Building." *The Architectural Review* 79 (January 1936): 10–12.

Richards, J.M. "Deconstruction and Reconstruction: A Theoretical Basis for Physical Planning." *The Architectural Review* 91. Part 1 (February 1942): 39–42. Part 2 (March 1942): 63–70.

Richards, J.M. "The Design Examined." *The Architectural Review* 85 (January 1939): 13–14.

Richards, J.M. "Highpoint Number Two: Tecton, Architects." *The Architectural Review* 84 (1938): 165–76.

Richards, J.M. "The Idea Behind the Idea." *The Architectural Review* 77 (May 1935): 207–16.

Richards, J.M. *Introduction to Modern Architecture*. Harmondsworth: Penguin, 1956 (1940).

Richards, J.M. *Memoirs of an Unjust Fella*. London: Weidenfeld & Nicolson, 1980.

Richards, J.M. "The Next Step?" *The Architectural Review* 107 (March 1950): 165–81.

Richards, J.M. "Wanted: An Hypothesis." *The Architectural Review* 90 (November 1941): 148–9.

Richards, J.M. and John Summerson, eds. *The Bombed Buildings of Britain: Second Edition Recording the Architectural Casualties Suffered During the Whole Period of Air Bombardment, 1940–45*. London: The Architectural Press, 1947.

Richards, J.M., Nikolaus Pevsner, H. de Cronin Hastings, and Osbert Lancaster. "The Second Half Century." *The Architectural Review* 101 (January 1947): 21–36.

Robbins, David, ed. *The Independent Group: Postwar Britain and the Aesthetics of Plenty*. Cambridge MA: The MIT Press, 1990.

Rogers, Ernesto. "The Phenomenology of European Architecture." In *A New Europe?*, edited by Stephen R. Graubard, 424–38. Boston: Beacon Press, 1964.

Rosenauer, Michael. "The House and the Town." *The Architectural Review* 64 (December 1928): 231–2.

Rosso, Michela. "John N. Summerson and Tales of Modern Architecture." *Journal of Architecture* 5 (Spring 2000): 65–89.

Rosso, Michela. *La storia utile: Patrimonio e modernità nel lavoro di John Summerson e Nikolaus Pevsner: Londra 1928–1955*. Torino: Edizioni di Comunita, 2001.

"The Royal Festival Hall." *Architects' Year Book* 4 (1951): 188–230.

Royal Institute of British Architects. *Towards a New Britain*. London: The Architectural Press, 1942.

Saint, Andrew. *Towards a Social Architecture: The Role of School Building in Postwar England*. New Haven and London: Yale University Press, 1987.

Saler, Michael. *The Avant-Garde in Interwar England: Medieval Modernism and the London Underground*. New York and Oxford: Oxford University Press, 1999

Samuel, Godfrey. "Radiant City and Garden Suburb: Corbusier's Ville Radieuse." *Journal of the Royal Institute of British Architects* 43 (April 4, 1936): 595–9.

Samuely, Felix. "Aspects of A.R.P." *Focus* 3 (Spring 1939): 48–52.

Samuely, Felix and Conrad W. Hamann. "Civil Defence: The Government's Policy for the A.R.P. Structures: An Analysis." *The Architects' Journal* 89 (June 1, 1939): 959–1018.

Sebald, W.G. *On the Natural History of Destruction.* Translated by Anthea Bell. London: Penguin, 2003 (1999).

Senter, Terence A. "Moholy-Nagy in England." MPhil thesis, University of Nottingham, 1977.

Shand, P.M. [Philip Morton]. "Scenario for a Human Drama." Seven-part article, *The Architectural Review (AR)* 76–7 (1934–5). Part I: "Foreword." *AR* 16 (July 1934): 9–16; Part II: "Immediate Background." *AR* 16 (August 1934): 39–42; Part III: "Peter Behrens." *AR* 16 (September 1934): 83–9; Part IV: "Van de Velde to Wagner." *AR* 16 (October 1934): 131–4; Part V: "Glasgow Interlude." *AR* 187 (January 1935): 23–6; Part VI: "Machine-à-Habiter to the House of Character." *AR* 11 (February 1935): 61–4. Part VII: "Looping the Loop." *AR* 77 (March 1935): 99–102.

Sharp, Dennis. "British Modern Architecture of the 30s." *A+U* 240 (September 1990): 37–50.

Sharp, Dennis. "Concept and Interpretation: The Aims and Principles of the MARS Plan London." *Perspecta* 13/14 (1971): 167.

Sharp, Dennis, ed. *Connell Ward Lucas: Modern Movement Architects in England 1929–1939.* London: Book Art, 1994.

Sharp, Dennis. "Framing the Welfare State." *Zodiac* 16 (November 1996): 56–75.

Sharp, Dennis. *Planning and Architecture: Essays Presented to Arthur Korn by the AA.* London: Architectural Association/Barrie and Rockcliff, 1967.

Smiles, Sam. *Going Modern and Being British: Art, Architecture, and Design in Devon c. 1910–1960.* Exeter: Royal Albert Museum, 1998.

Smithson, Alison. "Cluster City: A New Shape for the Community." *The Architectural Review* 122 (November 1957): 333–6.

Smithson, Alison, ed. *Team Ten Primer.* Cambridge, MA: The MIT Press, 1968.

Smithson, Alison, ed. *Team 10 Meetings: 1953–1984.* New York: Rizzoli, 1991.

Smithson, Peter. "The Idea of Architecture in the '50s." *The Architects' Journal* 131 (January 21, 1960): 121–6.

Smithson, Peter. Letter to the editor. *Architectural Design* 25 (November 1955).

Smithson, Peter. "Toulouse le Mirail," *Architectural Design* 41 (October 1971): 599–601.

Smithson, Alison and Peter. *Without Rhetoric: An Architectural Aesthetic 1955–1972.* London: Latimer, 1973.

Snow, C.P. *The Two Cultures.* Cambridge and New York: Cambridge University Press, 1998 (1959).

Snowman, Daniel. *The Hitler Émigrés: The Cultural Impact on Britain of Refugees from Nazism.* London: Chatto & Windus, 2002.

Solkin, David. "The British and the Modern." In *Towards a Modern Art World,* edited by Brian Allen, 1–6. New Haven: Yale University Press, 1995.

Soussloff, Catherine, ed. *Jewish Identity in Modern Art History.* Berkeley and Los Angeles: UCLA Press, 1999.

Spa Green Estate: Handbook for Tenants. London: Finsbury Borough Council, 1949.

Stamp, Gavin. *Britain in the Thirties.* London: Architectural Design, 1980.

Steiner, Hadas A. "For the Birds." *Grey Room* 13 (Fall 2003): 5–31.

Stratton, P.M. "The Line from France." *The Architectural Review* 64 (July 1928): 1–2.

Summerson, John. "Bread and Butter and Architecture." *Plan* 2 (1944): 4–7.

Summerson, John, ed. *Concerning Architecture: Essays on Architectural Writers and Writing presented to Nikolaus Pevsner.* London: Allen Lane/The Penguin Press, 1968.

Summerson, John. "How We Began: The Early History of the Architectural Association." *The Architect and Building News* (April 25, 1947): 74–9.

Summerson, John. "The MARS Group and the Thirties." In *English Architecture, Public and Private*, edited by John Bold and Edward Chaney, 303–10. London: The Hambledon Press, 1993.

Summerson, John. "The Past in the Future," lecture delivered at Bristol University in 1947 and reprinted in *Heavenly Mansions and Other Essays on Architecture*, edited by John Summerson, 219–42. New York: W.W. Norton and Company, 1998.

Summerson, John. "Ruins and the Future." *The Listener* 25 (April 17, 1941): 563–4.

Tafuri, Manfredo and Francisco Dal Co. *Modern Architecture*, 2 vols. Translated by Robert Erich Wolf. New York: M.H. Abrams, 1979 (Italian edition, 1976).

Tatton Brown, William and Aileen. "Three-Dimensional Town Planning." *The Architectural Review* 90 (September 1941): 82–8.

Taut, Bruno. *Modern Architecture.* London: The Studio, 1929.

Tecton. *Planned A.R.P.* London: The Architectural Press, 1939.

Thomson, Christina. "Contextualizing the Continental: The Work of German Émigré Architects in Britain, 1933–45." Ph.D. diss., University of Warwick, 1999.

Tigerman, Stanley. *The Architecture of Exile.* New York: Rizzoli International Publications, 1988.

Towndrow, Frederic. *Architecture in the Balance: An Approach to the Art of Scientific Humanism.* London: Chatto & Windus, 1933.

Towndrow, Frederic, ed. *Replanning Britain: A Summarized Report of the Oxford Conference of the Town and Country Planning Association.* London: Faber & Faber, 1941.

Trubowitz, Lara. *Civil Antisemitism, Modernism, and British Culture, 1902–1939.* New York: Palgrave Macmillan, 2012.

Tubbs, Ralph. *Living in Cities.* Harmondsworth: Penguin Books, 1942.

Unit One: The Modern Movement in English Architecture, Painting and Sculpture. London: Cassell, 1934. Includes introduction by Herbert Read.

Vago, Pierre. *Une vie intense.* Brussels: Editions AAM (Archives d'Architecture Moderne), 2000.

Warburton, Nigel. *Ernö Goldfinger: The Life of an Architect.* London: Routledge, 2003.

Wells, H.G. *Anticipations of the Reaction of Mechanical and Scientific Progress Upon Human Life and Thought.* London: Chapman & Hall, 1902.

Whiteley, Nigel. "Toward a Throwaway Culture: Consumerism, 'Style Obsolescence' and Cultural Theory in the 1950s and 1960s." *Oxford Art Journal* 10 (October 1987): 3–27.

Willett, John. "The Emigration and the Arts." In *Exile in Great Britain: Refugees from Hitler's Germany*, edited by Gerhard Hirschfeld, 195–217. Leamington Spa: Berg Publishers/The German Historical Institute; Atlantic Highlands: The Humanities Press, 1984.

Williams-Ellis, Clough. *England and the Octopus*. Portmeirion: Penrhyndeudraeth, 1928 [1975].

Yorke, F.R.S. *The Modern House*. London: The Architectural Press, 1934.

Yorke, F.RS. *The Modern House in England*. London: The Architectural Press, 1937.

Yorke, F.R.S. and Frederick Gibberd. *The Modern Flat*. London: The Architectural Press, 1937.

Yorke, F.R.S. and Penelope Whiting. *The New Small House*. London: The Architectural Press, 1953.

Young, Ken and Patricia L. Garside. *Metropolitan London: Politics and Urban Change 1837–1981*. London: Edward Arnold Publishers Ltd., 1982.

Zemel, Carol. *Looking Jewish: Visual Culture and Modern Diaspora*. Indianapolis: Indiana University Press, 2015.

Zevi, Bruno. *Eric Mendelsohn*. New York: Rizzoli, 1985.

Index

Note: Page numbers in italic type indicate illustrations.

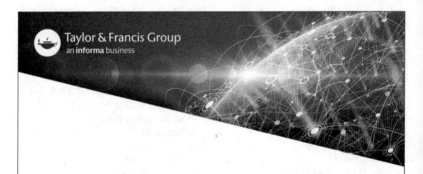